NORTHERN VERMONT
IN THE WAR OF 1812

NORTHERN VERMONT IN THE WAR OF 1812

— Jason Barney —

Published by The History Press
Charleston, SC
www.historypress.com

Copyright © 2019 by Jason Barney
All rights reserved

Front cover, bottom: Benson, *Lake Champlain, 1813*, 1813. Watercolor and graphite on woven paper, 9 3/4 x 14 13/16 inches. *Collection of Shelburne Museum, gift of J. Watson Webb Jr. 1964-60.1.*

First published 2019

Manufactured in the United States

ISBN 9781467141697

Library of Congress Control Number: 2019939739

Notice: The information in this book is true and complete to the best of our knowledge. It is offered without guarantee on the part of the author or The History Press. The author and The History Press disclaim all liability in connection with the use of this book.

All rights reserved. No part of this book may be reproduced or transmitted in any form whatsoever without prior written permission from the publisher except in the case of brief quotations embodied in critical articles and reviews.

This book is for the Barney family.

CONTENTS

Acknowledgements 9
Introduction: History in the Backyard 11

1. Setting the Stage: Natives, Colonials and Revolution 15
2. The Years before the Conflict: 1783–1811 24
3. Roads on the Border Lead to War: Winter 1811–Spring 1812 35
4. Swanton, A Cog in the War Machine: Summer 1812 42
5. There and Back Again: Fall 1812 57
6. War Is Cold and Unforgiving: Winter 1812–1813 71
7. The Calm before the Storm: Spring 1813 74
8. A Storm Hits the Northern Hub: Summer 1813 79
9. A Petty War along Lake Champlain: Fall 1813 98
10. Spheres of Influence: Winter 1813–1814 110
11. A Hub Once Again: Spring 1814 117
12. Vermont to the Rescue: Summer 1814 127
13. The End: Fall, Winter, Spring 1814–1815 147
14. The Present Day 148

Notes 151
Bibliography 163
Index 167
About the Author 173

ACKNOWLEDGEMENTS

Special thanks go to Mike Kinsella and The History Press for being interested in this story. My wife, Christine Eldred, deserves special recognition for supporting me during my morning writing time. She also was the beta reader for this manuscript and generously donated her time. Armand Messier of Northern Vermont Aerial Photography was also very generous with his time, and his pictures add a lot to this book. Lindsay DiDio deserves a lot of credit for coming up with some great images and squeezing in quick edits. I'd like to thank Scott McLaughlin and Elise Guyette for reminding me how cool history can be. I'd like to thank my son, Sam, for constant drives where Dad said, "You know there was a battle over there." I'd like to thank all the members of my family for offering words of encouragement. When any of them heard about this project, they each responded with pride: "We knew you had it in you, Jay."

Introduction

HISTORY IN THE BACKYARD

The central theme of this work is the discovery of untold history. My intent is to present this information so that northern Vermont gets its due credit. Other writers have put together the branches of the War of 1812 family tree, and one line just did not receive much attention. I hope what you are about to read comes across like the hidden details of a rarely looked at family photo album. Individual points can be examined and enjoyed, but multiple pieces can be woven together into a more concrete story.

Over the course of my interest in the War of 1812, I discovered the lure of research and how unanswered questions can take hold of my thinking. My first read of the War of 1812 was about as life-changing as eating the next meal. My information came from my history classes, where we spent less than a day on the War of 1812. Due to my love of history, I had glossed over the Swanton history book and skimmed the pages relating to the conflict. The War of 1812 just loses out to the Revolution, the Civil War and World War II. Entire units are devoted to those conflicts.

Meanwhile, my father and grandfather did on-and-off genealogy work, and my family was lucky enough to have had an ancestor write the first edition of the Swanton history book, written in 1886. I discovered our family line fought in the War of 1812, with two Barneys serving against the British. To the teenage mind, it was worth sharing with others, but there wasn't much interest. Barneys fought on the side of the colonials in the Revolution. Barneys died fighting to keep the country together during the Civil War.

The War of 1812 was…eh.

Introduction

"Bandstand Island," located in Missisquoi Bay. *Photo by Armand Messier of northernvermontaerial.com.*

It wasn't until my teaching career began in 2002 that I began to truly understand the historical significance of the area that I grew up in. As a young teacher, when I could, I threw in references about Swanton's history or local events related to national happenings. Well into my teaching career, while taking graduate-level history classes, is when I started to consider myself an amateur historian. I joined the Swanton Historical Society. Like the volunteer firemen of Vermont, these kind folks donated their time to the community, making sure museums were maintained and history preserved.

When I began those graduate courses ten years into my teaching career, it took only a few days to discover I was working on something that was much larger. Those wonderful classes were designed to foster historical inquiry. I devoured Vermont history books like Halloween candy. Soon my research morphed into an internship with the Swanton Historical Society, and I began some of the most fulfilling work of my professional teaching career.

What I discovered profoundly impacted what I squeezed into different lessons in my classroom, and I became the local history geek for the Social Studies Department. It wasn't every week, but other members of the department occasionally asked for help on a slideshow about Vermont in the Depression era and so on. In my own classroom, if I could spend time on

Introduction

Abenaki history, local Civil War letters or nearby Cold War missile silo sites, I felt like I was a better teacher.

Missisquoi Valley Union High School rewarded all of my geeky research and local history productivity by tweaking its course offerings and letting me develop a local history class. It ran one semester, in the spring of 2018. There were fifteen students. The class was not earth-shattering, but word of mouth was positive enough that in the fall of 2018–19 the school could normalize it into the schedule. There would be seven local history classes offered over the next two semesters.

The community was making the effort to pay attention to its own history.

Northwestern Vermont and the War of 1812 aren't totally unexplored, as they have been covered in a roundabout way by multiple historical texts. However, I was surprised to learn there was no single text on the subject matter. A lot of historical documentation exists that defines the importance of the Champlain Valley, the town of Swanton and the neighboring communities during the War of 1812. None of it had ever been brought together into one volume.

I do recall what I learned about the War of 1812 in school. In the elementary grades, the exposure was anchored to national events. The British forced American sailors on ships. Washington, D.C. was burned. Fort McHenry. "The Star-Spangled Banner." Maybe the Battle of New Orleans was covered. By high school, the exposure was a little more detailed, but it still wasn't more than a day or two of study. The Battle of Plattsburgh…and then we moved on…

It wasn't until my postgraduate work that my professional attention started to turn more toward local history. What I discovered altered my view of teaching, redefined my view of the area I grew up in and changed much of the information I gave to students.

The history of my home area wasn't just a few pages in someone else's history book. It deserved its own.

On many levels, I can't believe it has taken more than two centuries for this story to be told.

Here it is.

1
SETTING THE STAGE

Natives, Colonials and Revolution

Hubs are important.

The War of 1812 was fought from Detroit to New Orleans, from Washington, D.C., to the Canadian border. It was the North American continent's brief involvement in the Napoleonic Wars and saw the young nation renew its conflict with England. Swanton, Vermont, a small community in the northwest corner of the Green Mountain State, played a significant and, until recently, undiscovered role in that conflict.

In the Champlain Valley, the communities that receive the most War of 1812 attention are Plattsburgh, New York, and Burlington, Vermont. Burlington rests some forty miles south of the Canadian border on the east side of Lake Champlain. It was an important economic hub of activity before the war and became a nexus for the U.S. military during it. Between 1812 and 1815, troops trained, camped and prepared for war all around the area of Battery Park. At different times, American warships anchored in Burlington's waters. Plattsburgh, on the west side of the lake, has a much more visible association with the conflict. It was the launching point for numerous invasions of Quebec and was the temporary headquarters for the military in the theater. It was raided several times and was the location of one of the crucial battles of the war. Both communities suffered through harsh Valley Forge–like winters.

However, to fully understand the rich history of the central hubs like Burlington and Plattsburgh, smaller communities like Swanton, Vermont, deserve attention. To fully appreciate the details of the era, the stories of

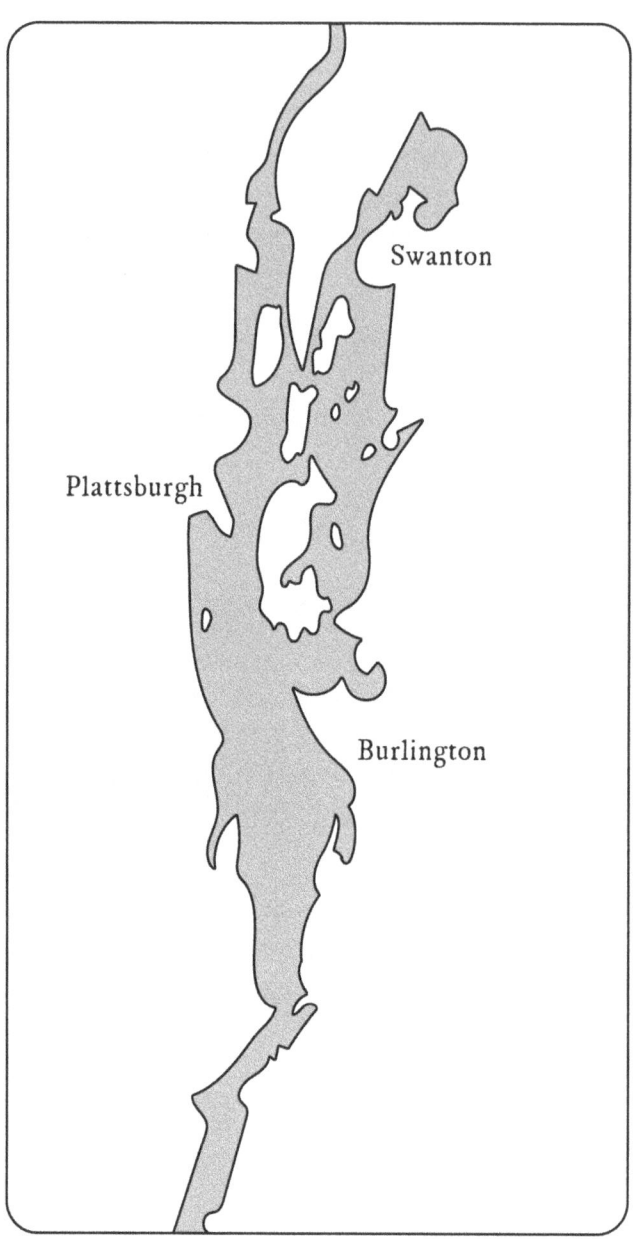

Swanton's location on Lake Champlain relative to the larger hubs of Burlington and Plattsburgh. *Artwork by Lindsay DiDio.*

"frontier" communities need more focus. Doing so gives a greater breadth of information, a more nuanced understanding of what occurred and better knowledge of how history unfolded.

Think of these two communities as the wagon wheels or train tracks for the American war effort in the region. Burlington, on the east shore of Lake Champlain, was located in a state that did not fully support the war. Plattsburgh was on the western shore, a little bit closer to the enemy at the Canadian border. It was the natural staging area for any assault against the British in Canada. If these two communities are the wheels, think of Lake Champlain as the road that allowed any assault to move north. For two hundred years, accounts of the early 1800s have given those communities their due credit.

There is a growing body of historical evidence allowing Swanton, northwestern Vermont and the communities along the Canadian border to take their rightful place as smaller hubs of activity during the period. It would be historically naïve to claim that Swanton and the surrounding area were ever as important as Burlington or Plattsburgh. However, the complete story of the war can't be told without acknowledging smaller hubs of activity. Centers of activity are important. They are focal points. A lot goes on around them. They are like the axles of a wheel, supporting a lot of pressure.

This is the story of the smaller communities. That story doesn't start with the summer war was declared; it starts much, much earlier.

The long colonial history of the northern Champlain Valley should be taken into account when discussing the lead up to the War of 1812. The battles, campaigns, raids and troop movements through the region are so numerous they are difficult to count. Native American history, the French and Indian Wars and the American Revolution all lead up to the period covered in this book.

There is a growing body of evidence that warfare existed in the area well before the arrival of white settlers in the region. When the French explorer Jacques Cartier visited the St. Lawrence Valley and the area of Montreal in 1534, there was evidence of regional conflict. The inhabitants, who called their settlement Hochelega—which later became Montreal—had experienced enough hostility from tribes to the southwest that they had erected a palisaded fort around their longhouses.[1] The hostility came from the aggressive Iroquois in central New York; they made enough war that European explorers heard stories about Iroquois war parties.

As history unfolded and more whites explored the area, the amount of warfare increased. When the second French explorer, Samuel de Champlain, visited the area of Montreal in the early 1600s, the cultural landscape had totally changed. The group that Cartier likely contacted about seventy years prior had been wiped out. The native peoples he did encounter—the Montagnais, Micmac and others—communicated stories of warfare originating to the southwest. Champlain allied himself with the natives he encountered.

By the summer of 1609, the new allies ventured south along the Richelieu River into Lake Champlain, and history recorded the first European military action in the Champlain Valley. Champlain brought his small fleet of canoes right down the river, passing locations that would become military outposts over the next couple of hundred years. In early July, he passed the locations presently identified on the map as Rouses Point, New York, and Alburgh, Swanton and Isle La Motte, Vermont. When he reached the southern half of the lake, the Iroquois presented themselves. The events of this story are infamous, with Champlain discharging his arquebus and changing the flow of history. Conflict continued in the area through 1610 and later wars. The Abenaki, who inhabited the area of northwestern Vermont going back thousands of years, had a village on the banks of the Missisquoi River near Swanton when French fur traders followed Champlain after 1609. French missionaries no doubt visited the waterway in the late seventeenth century, and a French mission may have been established on the river in the early 1700s.

And it continued. Northern New England was on the periphery of the conflicts between France and England throughout the decades. Raids, skirmishes, battles, naval movements and retreats. They happened time and again.

The French in Quebec established a series of forts along the Richelieu River to protect against English-supported Iroquois raids. In 1666, they decided to extend their defensive efforts as far south as Isle La Motte. They built a fort along the western edge of the island, which was used to support their own raids against the Mohawks in upstate New York. These events would be a prelude to King Philip's War, a series of conflicts between Indians and colonists. Abenaki from Vermont participated in attacks against English settlers all throughout New England, and Lake Champlain became a military superhighway for raiding parties north and south.

Not much later, it was Queen Anne's War. The Champlain Valley was the local theater for a much larger conflict, with Europe embroiled in the War of the Spanish Succession. Tension between native tribes boiled over, aided by the constant aggression and territorial expansion of the English and French settlers. The water between what is today New York and Vermont was once again a critical travel conduit for those inflicting damage north and south.

A little-known conflict in the middle of the 1720s was anchored in what is today Swanton, Vermont. This struggle is not directly linked to a major conflict in Europe but does stress the unique history of northern Lake Champlain. The Abenaki chief Greylock refused to submit to English encroachment along the already diminishing Abenaki frontier and engaged in raids against their northernmost settlements. The same tensions boiled over in Maine, resulting in what is known as Father Rawles' War. Based at a palisaded fort along the Missisquoi River in Swanton, Greylock led dozens of warriors in long journeys by canoe over the waters of Lake Champlain. They raided all the way into Massachusetts. The French remained neutral in this entanglement, but such conflicts brought the French to believe they needed more forward bases to protect Montreal and Quebec. Such fortifications would enable them to keep the British in southern New England at bay. As early as 1731, they set up a small fort on the eastern side of Lake Champlain, at Chimney Point. Not long afterward, they moved to the western side of the lake and constructed Crown Point.

King George's War, fought between 1744 and 1748, further identifies the growing military importance of the region. French settlements are recorded in northern Vermont throughout this period, with a settlement in Swanton concretely dated to this time. At this juncture, the French and English decision makers, those responsible for the implementation of the war machine, decided to think much bigger. It wasn't enough to raid or harass enemy settlements hundreds of miles away. Conquering the enemy's colonies and vanquishing their authority on the continent emerged as larger goals.

New France was at a decided disadvantage against the much more populated New England colonies. Keeping the English distant became the primary defensive mindset, and it was decided a large forward operating base was the best countermeasure against encroachment from the south. Construction on Fort Carillon began in the middle of the 1750s. The ambitiousness of the operation showed what was at stake. War between the English and French, the colonials from both sides and their native allies had already been waged three times. And so the next conflict was fought.

With the onset of the French and Indian War, the intensity was brought to an all new level. French settlements were scattered north of Fort Ticonderoga in northern Vermont and along the Richelieu River. The original Swanton settlement had grown considerably. Misled by a few years of peace, the local Abenaki population had grown. The French investment in the northeastern tier of Lake Champlain was extensive. Beyond the mission and mill erected at some point in the 1740s, the French military invested in a palisaded fort once war approached.[2] The settlements along Missisquoi Bay were the halfway point between French settlements to the north and Fort Carillon to the south. It would have been an attractive layover spot for military units and supply convoys. Based on the intensity of the activity throughout the 1740s and 1750s, it is also reasonable to speculate the settlement had the necessary docks to support the larger vessels being constructed to sail the lake. French colonists in Missisquoi Bay would have been involved in supplying the troops at the southern end of the lake.[3]

However, France's fortunes in the New World were not in the hands of the people who lived here. Events in Europe had a major impact on the colonial empires, and all was not going well for the French. England was able to send far more military resources to the Americas, and France was not able to provide adequate forces to defend its interests across the Atlantic. Britain was willing to apply pressure where it had the advantage. The British armies were doing well in Europe, and the English navy was the best in the world. Where King Philip's War, Queen Anne's War and King George's War had ended with mixed results, the military events of the 1750s revealed England could apply pressure, especially in the North American colonies.

France's disadvantages in Europe had monstrous consequences for the French colonies in the Americas. In ways large and small, those events caused flash points all along the northern Champlain Valley. There is some evidence that the British targeted the Missisquoi settlement sometime in 1757 or 1758 with a raid specifically meant to prevent the community from supporting the larger French war effort.[4] In 1759, as the British and colonial forces inched ever closer to defeating the French, a bold raid was planned by Robert Rogers. Most of the French and Abenaki at Missisquoi had retreated to the French military base at Isle Aux Noix, just twelve miles away, on the Richelieu River. Many of the Abenaki either joined the French on the island fortification or removed themselves north to the village of Odanak. The British managed to bypass the French defenses and patrols, pass undetected into Missisquoi Bay and embark on what history remembers as Rogers' Raid.

Further evidence of the early importance of the area played out later in that war. With the southern portions of Lake Champlain, including Fort

Carillon (renamed Ticonderoga) under English control, the Crown looked to expel France's control of northern New England and Quebec. The British finally advanced northward, and the French desperately attempted to hold on to their colonies. Vessels of the French navy used the Missisquoi River delta to hide from the more powerful British navy. When the British did move down the lake, the entire army of several thousand men and their Lake Champlain navy sailed just to the west of present-day Alburgh. When the colonies of New France collapsed, they became an extension of England's global empire.

This conquest led to the American Revolution, the closest historical conflict directly related to the contents of this book.

The events of the American War for Independence that are anchored specifically in northern Vermont are rare, but they do bear mentioning. Prior to 1775, the population of the region was quite low. The French had moved miles to the north. Most of the Abenaki remained to the north as well. They no doubt felt safer on lands their ancestors had occupied and closer to the French, rather than exposed to English families they had fought against. Set away from the larger English colonies along the Atlantic, the Champlain Valley was the frontier. Massachusetts, New York and New Hampshire all lay claim to the area. The desires of New York and New Hampshire were the most serious and brought considerable tension. English colonists and land speculators did not want to risk purchasing property from one colony when another was promoting the very same tracts to its own colonists. As the larger events of 1775 approached, fewer than two hundred Englishmen lived in Swanton.[5]

The Revolution began with the Battles of Lexington and Concord on April 19, 1775. At that point, not all of the thirteen colonies were on board with full rebellion, but momentum built and events unfolded to the far north. Benedict Arnold, Ethan Allen and the Green Mountain Boys had stealthily crossed the southern areas of Lake Champlain by late May. After the fall of Fort Ticonderoga, the next act of the young rebellion on the lake was to seize the schooner of one of the prominent New York Loyalist families, the Skeenes.[6] Just days later, after quickly arming the vessel, Benedict Arnold was off the coast of present-day Alburgh, sailing into the Richelieu River, attempting to get the jump on the British forces at Isle Aux Noix and St. Jean, Quebec. The raid was successful. Arnold captured what became the second vessel in the small but growing American navy. The ambitious Americans sailed southward and passed Alburgh and Isle La Motte. Ethan Allen and his Green Mountain Boys were in the region at the same time.

At this point, the area of Missisquoi Bay was quiet. The loyalties of the people living right on the border may never be known, but the business interests of one Simon Metcalf have been recorded in some detail. Metcalf was likely a Loyalist. Economically speaking, he was aligned with the markets around Montreal and the English military installations along the Richelieu River. He owned a sawmill on one of the small islands at the mouth of the Missisquoi River, in the isolated confines of Missisquoi Bay.

American fleets returned to the northern edge of Lake Champlain within months. As soon as the Continental Congress gave its blessings to the overall war effort, the Champlain Valley once again became the main north–south travel route. By August 1776, American forces poured north on Lake Champlain, just west of present-day Grand Isle County. The overall objective of the invasion of Canada was to expel the British army from North America. This effort was made in conjunction with Benedict Arnold's bold strike through the Maine wilderness. The immediate American goals were to evict the enemy from Isle Aux Noix, the base just up the Richelieu River, only twelve miles from present-day Swanton and Highgate. As the American assault moved north and approached St. Jean, more and more men and equipment were just a rowboat ride away from northwestern Vermont.

Ben Franklin and other colonial dignitaries traveled the same route not long afterward. The effort was to evaluate the American fighting force in Canada, which was having problems, and to ascertain if the Quebec citizens of Franco descent could be convinced to join the rebellion. Franklin's mission ended abruptly, partly because the desperate American invasion of Canada collapsed around Quebec City. By the late spring of 1777, the American army was in full retreat, passing by the same locations it had conquered barely a year before.

At this point, the area became a no man's land between competing armies. The new forces from England had been responsible for repelling the American invasion, and a further build-up was planned to squash the rebellion in the north. An arms race erupted on Lake Champlain, and northern Vermont fell into both colonial and royal spheres of influence. The Americans, based at Fort Ticonderoga, desperately cobbled together a fleet to hold Lake Champlain and give the fledgling revolution a chance to survive. The British threw resources, men and materiel into a massive shipbuilding effort on the Richelieu River, just a stone's throw from Missisquoi Bay. By the summer of 1777, both sides were pouring massive amounts of effort into the coming fight.

In the end, the experienced British naval capabilities won out. They launched a massive force on Lake Champlain. In the days prior to the British assault in October, Arnold's small navy was in the region again, just off from Alburgh, attempting to bottle up the enemy navy before it could use its superior numbers and seize control of the area's most important waterway.

On October 11, 12 and 13, 1777, the rebel navy was defeated in a long retreating action. It was a victory of sorts for the Americans though, as the British didn't want to sustain an invasion force in the field through winter. They would delay their invasion until the spring of 1778.

When the ice melted the following year, the large English naval force moved south. Within sight of the northern Vermont coast, the largest fleet ever to occupy the lake sailed south. American resistance crumbled until the lengthy Saratoga campaign played out. While the Battle of Saratoga is recognized as one of the great battles in American history, the smaller conflicts of Hubbardton and Bennington involved many, many Green Mountain Boys.

The Revolution dragged on until 1783, but the rapid events of 1775–78 on Lake Champlain came to a close. When the British forces did surrender, there was a mass exodus of Tories to Canada. Large numbers of Loyalists used Lake Champlain as their departure route from the new country, not wanting to give up allegiance to the Crown. While the forces were limited, British soldiers maintained positions on the west side of Missisquoi Bay, in Alburgh and within the extreme northeast corner of New York until American settlers entered the area in the late 1780s.[7] The borderland after the Revolution was not clearly defined until Vermont achieved statehood in 1791.

So, prior to the War of 1812, the area had a long history of conflict. As the early years of the nineteenth century unfolded, a unique situation developed along the northern border. Canada, an English territory, had its southern regions populated by Americans who had chosen not to fight against the king and by French settlers willing to tolerate English rule. Despite the Revolution, a strong economy had developed in which former enemies openly traded and profited from developing markets.

2

THE YEARS BEFORE THE CONFLICT

1783–1811

Swanton is situated less than six miles from the Canadian border. The northeastern boundary of Lake Champlain, which opens up into the isolated Missisquoi Bay, is less than ten miles from water routes critical to eighteenth- and nineteenth-century shipping. The Missisquoi River rambles through northwest Vermont and was the most important artery of trade for towns like Highgate, Sheldon, Franklin, Enosburgh, Berkshire and Richford. Goods often found their way to Canadian markets after passing through Swanton. French Canadian customers valued Vermont potash, timber, beef and other commodities.

People tend to go where work and opportunities present themselves. Swanton was a prime example. After the Revolutionary War, fewer than 200 people lived there. By the 1810 census, there were over 1,600. It was as large as Burlington, rivaling the population of towns settled generations earlier, and was economically critical to Franklin County.

The borderland status of northwest Vermont defined why trade was so important at the time. The English-governed Canadian colonies were so interested in Vermont products that in 1788 they began to allow the free importation of products from the region.[8] Some of this was politically based, in that Vermont had not yet emerged from under the wing of the other colonies, to pseudo-independent status, to inching toward statehood. Within the United States, geographically Boston and New York were the obvious centers for trade, but the Champlain Valley was isolated—transporting goods such distances was extremely cost-prohibitive. Products took weeks

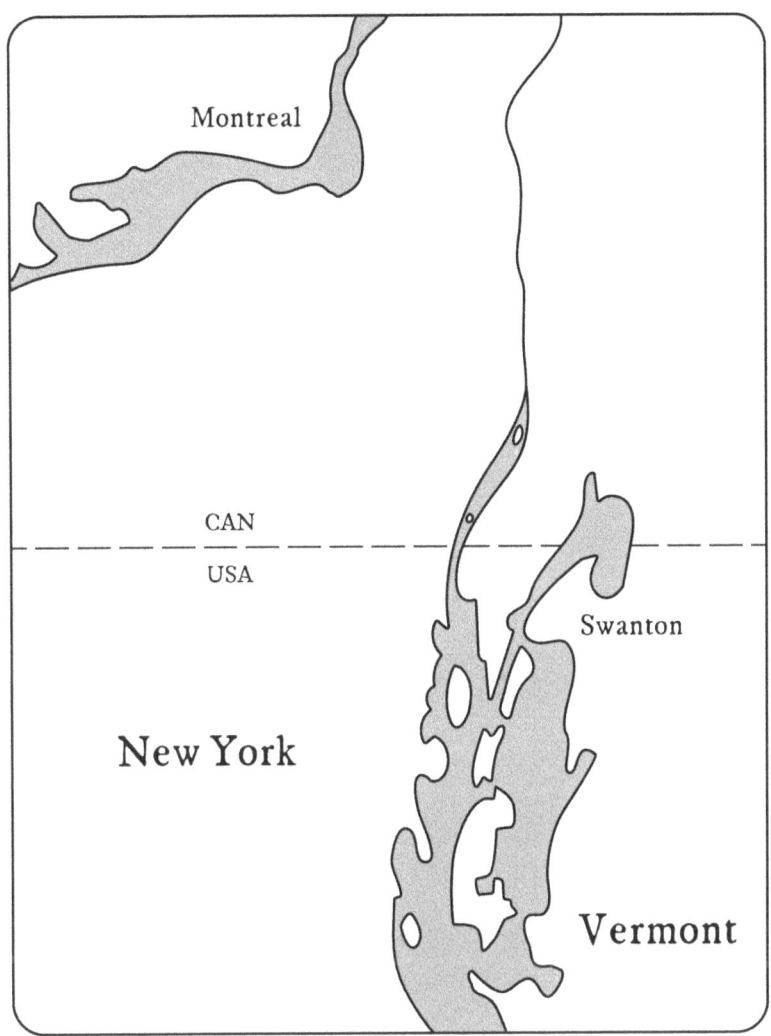

Swanton's proximity to the border and Canada. *Artwork by Lindsay DiDio.*

or longer to go over land routes. The north–south route along the Hudson River wasn't much better. Montreal and Quebec City were more accessible to Vermonters than the ports to the south.

 Potash and timber were the two main items for trade, although the market was certainly broad enough for other products. Both were incredibly valuable in England at the start of the Industrial Revolution. For the nineteenth-century world, potash was very important. It could be used in dyes, to make glass, paper and soap and was used during the processing of cloth and fabrics. Potash was available and gathered by Vermont merchants involved with the state's massive wood reserves. Creating potash involved refining burned wood or ashes in a large container. There were holes in the bottom, so water could be poured over the ashes and then leached into a gathering basin. A boiling period followed, and when the complex process was completed, the resulting product was available on the market. It was worth enough to prompt many Vermonters to turn their heads away from their countrymen. Vermont's abundant forests were a rich resource for the potash trade. By one estimate, there was such an abundance of trees and potash-related products that Burlington, Vermont, was the third-largest timber port in the United States by 1810.[9]

By the early 1800s, Swanton had become a blossoming community and was home to several growing businesses. Prior to national politics tangling with Vermonters' ability to trade with neighbors north of the forty-fifth parallel, the Missisquoi River was a pumping economic artery. A gristmill had been erected on the east side of the river. At least two sawmills processed timber floating from land-locked towns farther east. An iron forge had been erected around the turn of the century. Economically minded traders brought their potash to the banks of the Missisquoi, where it typically made its way to Montreal markets. A lime kiln, a marble mill, a woolen mill, a clothing store and various farming endeavors all brought economic opportunity to the Canadian border. By 1810, four separate ferries operated between Alburgh and Swanton.[10] A road connecting the village of Swanton to Maquam Bay was completed sometime in the late summer or early fall of 1811 by resident Levi Scott. A toll bridge was constructed over the southern leg of the Missisquoi River, more easily connecting Swanton with the large community of St. Albans, five miles away.

The grand scheme of events that brought the United States and England to war had a significant impact in the Champlain Valley. England controlled Canada and at times considered the Great Lakes region a possible "homeland" for an American Indian nation. U.S. encroachment westward only raised tensions. Also, America complained about the British policy of impressment, the forced service of American sailors onto British vessels in the Atlantic. This was highlighted by the Chesapeake-Leopard affair, where shots were exchanged at sea.

To avoid war, American politicians in Washington attempted to steer a course of neutrality, doing whatever possible to avoid potential military conflict with France or England. The legal aspects of this policy involved trade laws like Macon's Bill No. 2, the Embargo Acts and the Non-Intercourse Act of 1809. Each of these, in one way or another, limited trade with England, including British-controlled Canada.

In the Champlain Valley, the reaction to these federal laws was largely negative. While open rebellion did not exist on the border, smuggling blossomed, and political and economic tensions dramatically increased. As a matter of national policy, politicians tried to prevent England from benefiting from American goods. However, such policies devastated local economies. With the passage of each restrictive trade law, the market for goods produced in communities like Swanton declined substantially. If the locals couldn't sell their products, especially after impressive amounts of manual labor had been used to bring those products to market, people's wallets were hit hard.

Between 1807 and the official declaration of war in June 1812, Swanton and northwestern Vermont became a central hub for smuggling goods to Canadian markets. One of the reasons why the population of Vermont exploded between 1791 and 1810 was the economic atmosphere. The value of the goods transported to the Richelieu River through St. Jean increased nearly ten times between 1775 and the first decade of the nineteenth century.[11] When Washington ordered that no citizen or business could conduct transactions with Canada, it was like telling an infant to stop growing. Growth was bound to happen, regardless of the desires of the federal government.

The federal government attempted to regulate and monitor activity over and through the border primarily through the establishment of customshouses. Prior to 1804, the customshouse on Lake Champlain was located on South Hero, in the center of the northern portion of the lake, but still far from Canada.[12] Its location just a few miles from Burlington in the post–Revolutionary War period is understandable. Its placement was probably related to the proximity to Burlington and the knowledge that the British still maintained blockhouses on Lake Champlain just to the north.

For a town like Swanton, which had the mills, lumberyards and port access with its neighbors to the north, the customshouse twenty miles south was probably ignored by many. Merchants would not have wanted to venture south to check with the government prior to doing business with the Canadians. Swanton's population was a tiny 71 individuals in 1791, the year of Vermont statehood. By 1800, it was 858.[13] Other communities in Franklin County saw similar growth. Highgate, just to the northeast but with less lake access, saw its numbers quadruple from over 100 in 1791 to more than 400 in 1800. Sheldon, directly to Swanton's east, saw its population explode from 40 people to well over 400. St. Albans, the largest town north of Burlington today and directly south of Swanton, saw its population blossom from over 200 in 1791 to more than 900. Alburgh, the northwesternmost town in Vermont, doubled its population from 400 to nearly 800. Clearly, there was a lot of economic activity and growth along the border.

On the national level, Jefferson's desire to keep the United States from becoming embroiled in European conflicts was not without merit. While England and France were engaged in the Napoleonic Wars, the United States was given breathing room and a chance to grow. The local boom in economic activity was in part aided by commerce with both warring nations. However, keeping America neutral was a difficult task, especially with the vengeful attitude of the British Empire. A growing concern became the issue of impressment, where American seamen were seized in open waters by the English navy. During these stops, England believed it had the power to take seamen who had once served the Crown and return them to service. Americans were understandably incensed, because many were British immigrants themselves. Tensions really came to a boil in 1807, with the Chesapeake-Leopard affair. The USS *Chesapeake* was stopped, fired upon and boarded by the HMS *Leopard*. Members of the American crew were wounded, and three sailors were taken by the British. War was avoided at the cost of American pride. Adding to the growing tensions was the belief the British would try to unite the continent's native tribes to the west.

In 1804, the Lake Champlain customshouse was moved to Windmill Point in Alburgh; that location presented a much better area to monitor activity. The previous location at the southern tip of Grand Isle County allowed that land mass to function as a sword cutting through government authority. By moving the customshouse to Alburgh, the government pulled a sheath over the sharpness of hidden economic activity. The eastern portion of Lake Champlain, north of Burlington, features generally shallow waters. The western side is deeper and provides the main water route north to the Richelieu River of Canada. A customshouse in Alburgh made perfect sense, to some people.

In order to enforce the wishes of President Jefferson and Congress, the federal government needed boots on the ground and sails on the lake. Between the time of the relocation of the customshouse in 1804 and commencement of increased enforcement by federal officials in 1808, only a handful of agents worked in the area. Jabez Penniman is the most well-known. However, there were others. For a time, Samuel Buell was an assistant collector. In

1805, Nathan B. Haswell was another. Daniel Stanniford, a law enforcement officer in Chittenden County, worked with customs inspectors.[14] They were not just needed for the open waters of Champlain; in the lead up to the embargo, multiple ferries had been established over the thinner portions of the Missisquoi Bay area, each of them anchoring with Alburgh to the west.[15]

The relocation of the customshouse to the north and the arrival of more agents did little to impact the moneymaking operations the federal government was up against. Penniman, in Swanton in January 1808, urged other customs agents to use extreme caution.[16] His warnings appropriately identified the pressure that was building. The harder the government pushed, the more the smugglers were likely to push back. They were increasing their efforts to get around the law, regardless of national policies. Controlling contraband shipping in Missisquoi Bay in the spring of 1808 was problematic at best.[17]

Along with Penniman, Vermont's political establishment was having difficulty coming to grips with enforcing Jefferson's embargo. Governor Israel Smith called up a small company of militia from St. Albans to maintain a presence along the Canadian border. While many towns were engaged in maintaining and drilling their militia units, on May 4, 1808, eighteen men from St. Albans under the command of Heman Hawkins were called up for active duty in Swanton and Alburgh.[18]

June was always the key month for town militia units to organize and train. Notes in several town histories mention the work and drilling during late spring and early summer. Like volunteer service in local fire departments, the training was semiregular and happened every year. Militias organized themselves early in June, usually on the first Tuesday of the month. The Town of St. Johnsbury's history provides a glimpse into militia duties of the time.

The township had been involved in organizing militia activities for more than fifty years, and members of the light infantry were warned to gather at Captain French's Hotel, armed and equipped for military service. This was the normal activity of any town militia and unrelated to the call-up underway in St. Albans. Equipment was inspected, and each man had a musket, bayonet, ramrod, cartridges, bullets, cleaning supplies and a knapsack. While the training organized able-bodied men into a fighting force for a stateside emergency, some years the training was not as extensive as others.[19]

Back in western Vermont, the arrival of the militia on the border did little to stem the tide of illegal activity flowing north. Penniman noted that rafts were still getting through. In some cases, the tensions between local smugglers and the militia were heightened by Canadian men descending across the border to protect their own economic interests. Smaller militia units were effectively bullied and threatened to not get in the way. Some arrests were made, and at times contraband was seized. In the middle of May 1808, a Canadian newspaper reported that even with an armed gunboat, the militia and multiple customs agents in New York and Vermont, traffic was not being stopped.[20] Within a few weeks, a second detachment of militia from St. Albans, another twenty-five-man unit under the command of Lieutenant John Whittemore, was on its way for patrol in Swanton and Alburgh.[21] Even with two companies at the border, the embargo was ineffective. Newspapers from southern Vermont speculated about the effectiveness of the militia from towns so close to the border and questioned if they could perform their duties. Ineffectiveness of the first two companies only increased the scrutiny and efforts of law enforcement. In late May, Rutland County was asked to provide multiple companies totaling at least 150 men. Some would be replacements; most were being used to increase the government's presence. It was an escalation that continued throughout the rest of the spring and into the summer with deadly consequences.[22]

The most famous of these are the exploits of the *Black Snake*, a ship with a single mast that carried scores of barrels of potash illegally into Canada on a regular basis.[23] The federal government had a revenue cutter, the *Fly*, available on the open lake. As the government attempted to tighten its grip on illegal activity, smugglers began employing vessels that could simply evade government craft. Some rafts were detained at the mouth of the Richelieu River, but this dealt with only the lumber trade, and not all were being stopped. Barrels of potash were not easily transported on rafts, so vessels like the *Black Snake* came into play. Originally a ferryboat used between Charlotte, Vermont, and Essex, New York, prior to the embargo, it had one mainsail, was forty feet long and fourteen feet wide and employed oars to help navigate the shallow, swampy waters of the Missisquoi River delta. The *Black Snake* carried as many as one hundred barrels of potash into Canadian waters each trip. History does not record exactly when the *Black Snake* began to make its illegal runs, but it was probably around the time that the St. Albans and Rutland militias were called up. Other smuggling boats attempted to evade the gunboat and revenue cutters, and in the final days of May and the first days of June 1808, at least four sloops or bateaux were seized with barrels of potash while moving north. Some of the Rutland County men were in Swanton by June 5 and were ordered to patrol the roads for wagons moving toward Quebec.[24] Two companies of the new arrivals were ordered to Windmill Point and experienced the frustration and danger that Penniman had speculated about only months prior. The further into the summer the area got, the more the border agents had to deal with.

By the middle of June, it was clear that even the additional companies were not going to be altogether effective. On June 9, orders arrived in Swanton for squads of soldiers and cavalry to depart for suspected illegal activity in St. Albans, Hinesburg and Georgia. On June 10, customs officers and militia attempted to deal with rafts moving north, probably destined for Caldwell's Manor, on the northwest portion of Missisquoi Bay in Canada. They also tried to deal with another raft in the vicinity of Isle La Motte.[25] It was stopped and seized by the militia, but local smugglers confronted law enforcement. In this instance, gunfire was exchanged but no blood spilled.

The situation became so dangerous that desertion hit the ranks of the militia. Servicemen noted the promised supplies were not available, and the constant futility of patrolling the border had an ill effect on morale. Adding to the difficulties of enforcement, the black-market activity was supported by the local population. Additionally, tensions built between the Rutland and St. Albans militia units when members of the St. Albans contingent were accused of not being up to the task.[26] Federal agents were ordered to the area as well.[27] Still, Penniman found it nearly impossible to deal with the illegal trade.

By the last week of June, events were heading in the general direction of confrontation. Lieutenant Bennett, with a squad of sixteen federal soldiers, arrived in northern Vermont at about the same time that the government contracted with private ship owners for additional transport on the lake. The schooner, *Beaver*, and the sloop, *Juno*, were brought into service to transport federal supplies north to Swanton Falls and Windmill Point from southern locations. (The *Juno* would later come into the service of the government during the War of 1812.) At about the same time, owners of active smuggling ships invested in weapons and men who would protect their desire for profit. The *Black Snake* was operating in the swampy waters of the Missisquoi River delta, and members of its crew were investigating purchasing guns to counter the increased presence of the government.[28] The push and shove between law and order and the smugglers escalated further when a group of men stole the government revenue cutter stationed at Windmill Point as June came to an end.[29]

Early July brought more problems. Many Vermonters depended on agriculture for survival, and members of the militia were no different.

Crops needed to be cultivated given the time of year, and another thirteen militiamen simply left their assignment and returned home to work on their farms.[30] Such holes in government enforcement allowed boats like the *Black Snake* to make successful runs north and south.

In August that changed.

Revenue agents were able to collect enough information on the activities of the *Black Snake* that law enforcement zeroed in on its activity. Penniman and the federal government had the opportunity to eliminate one of the lake's more notorious black-market vessels, and a high level of attention was given to bringing the *Snake* in. Agents became aware it was again in the vicinity of the Missisquoi Bay on August 1. Penniman traveled to Windmill Point to organize the effort to track down and seize the *Black Snake*. In order to completely the tighten the noose, he ordered Lieutenant Farrington and twelve members of the detachment there to man the revenue cutter *Fly*. The next day, the *Fly* moved along the southern tip of Alburgh into the waters of Maquam Bay and then north into Missisquoi Bay. The *Fly* and its crew missed the *Black Snake* by less than a day, as the smugglers had moved just a few miles south, along the eastern shore of the Lake Champlain islands. Their destination was the Winooski River, where they planned to go inland to obtain another load of potash.

August 3 was the day when government agents had the opportunity to pick off the big fish. Seizing the *Black Snake* would be a tangible victory. It would show the public that the efforts of the government were not in vain, and that the militia, federal soldiers and revenue agents were able to enforce federal law.

The smugglers were considering their own form of escalation. The crew had purchased a larger gun to protect their cargo and planned for the possibility of armed confrontation. As word spread among sympathetic landowners that the *Fly* was making its way up the Winooski River to capture the *Black Snake*, the smugglers became aware of the dwindling prospects of escape.

Lieutenant Farrington and the crew of the *Fly* came up the river, knowing they had the *Black Snake* cornered. At first nothing happened when Farrington ordered his crew to seize the smuggling ship. But when the revenue agents attempted to depart with their prize, shots were fired; two revenue agents and a local militia officer ended up dead. It was a story that grabbed national attention, and the government had received a blunt message about how far some locals were willing to go to protect their interests.

The resulting prosecution of those responsible for the death of the border agents consumed much of the state during the late summer and early fall of

1808. Despite the tensions, there was a general acceptance that the federal government had the authority to enforce federal laws. Consequently, the government had the legal authority to put the *Black Snake* smugglers on trial for their actions. Most of the men involved in the incident served prison time, and Cyrus B. Dean of Swanton was publicly executed. Thousands of Vermont citizens attended the hanging in Burlington's Battery Park.[31]

Historical accounts suggest the level of smuggling did not subside much during the years following the *Black Snake* affair. Samuel Buell was still stationed on Windmill Point throughout 1809.[32] The government was active on the lake with the *Lark* and the *Fly*, and along with occasional use of the gunboats, the overall effort was like trying to grab fish from out of a moving stream. Penniman's retirement in 1811 allowed Buell to be promoted to inspector of revenue for the region. James Wood and other officials remained on duty during the period. The smuggling turned deadly once again in the fall of 1811 when a skiff failed to check in with border agents. When the revenue cutter offered pursuit and the skiff still attempted to flee, gunshots were fired, resulting in the death of one smuggler.[33]

Although laws prohibited trade with America's European adversaries, the waters of the lake were quite active, even years into the embargo. In 1811, the customshouse in Champlain, New York, recorded trips and documented stops by multiple large vessels. One of the crafts that docked

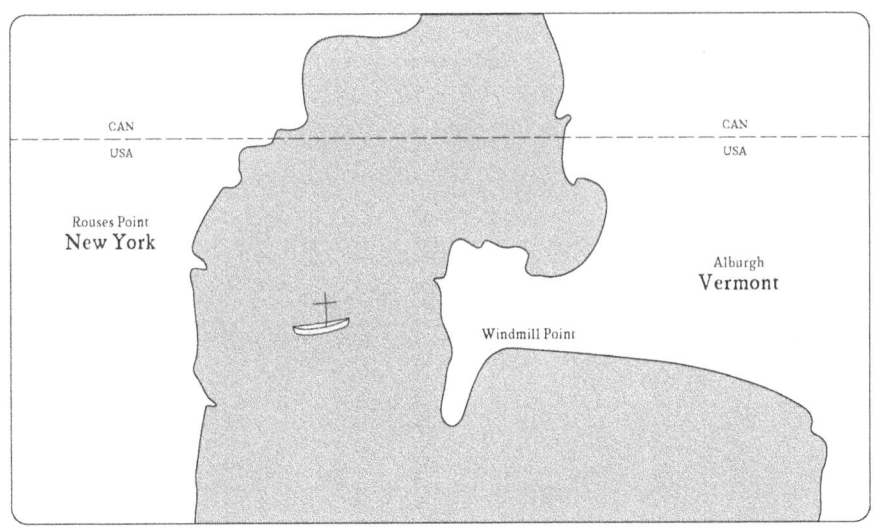

Windmill Point's proximity to the border made it a natural location for monitoring trade over the border. *Artwork by Lindsay DiDio.*

View of Windmill Point in Alburgh looking north. Canada is in the background. *Photo by Armand Messier of northernvermontaerial.com.*

at Champlain for inspection was the steamship *Vermont*. Another was the old English naval schooner *Liberty*, which often used St. Jean as its home port. Others were the sloops or merchant vessels *Eagle, Euretta, Jupiter, Hunter, Independence, Juno, Champlain, Essex, Rising Son, Mars, Enterprise, Lady Washington* and the *Richard*.[34] Another sloop operating in the embargo period was the fifty-ton *Saucy Fox*, owned by Gideon King in 1810.[35] It may have been linked to smuggling activity.[36]

3

ROADS ON THE BORDER LEAD TO WAR

WINTER 1811–SPRING 1812

Elements of the military were asked to work the border again in 1810 and 1811.[37] On the national level, relations between England and the United States continued to crumble. By early 1812, there was a sense that war was inevitable, often championed by the sections of the country farthest from English influence. Before the shooting started, the United States probably believed it was in a pretty good strategic and political position. The colonies had already declared independence from the British Empire only a generation before. The nation had quickly grown from the original thirteen colonies and enjoyed territorial expansion on a yearly basis. Before the ink of the Constitution was dry, Vermont had been admitted to the union, followed by multiple larger states to the west. England was an entire ocean away and waging an incredibly costly and long conflict with Napoleon's France. While the realities and bloodshed of war were not being discounted, the only true threat in the region was England's presence in Canada. In fact, American leadership saw possible expansion to the north as a benefit if war did occur. The Canadian provinces were very much the same as the territory in the great American West. Vast. Open. Lightly populated. If the British Empire could be divested of its holdings in Canada, as it almost had been during the American Revolution, the young country might never feel directly threatened by the empire again. Prior to 1812, American leadership believed taking Canada would be a relatively easy task. On numerous instances, Jefferson spoke of the United States simply taking Canada from England—while at the same time promoting the idea of staying out of European affairs altogether.[38]

The reality of any major threat from the north, however, did not really exist. British Canada had fewer than one million people. The growing United States had more than eight million. As war loomed, Sir George Prévost was the governor general of Canada, and he launched a few initiatives in light of the growing tensions. Those preparations proved to be insightful, especially with a much stronger America eyeing war. First, Prévost had to deal with the cultural differences inside the land he was about to defend. The colony had originally been set up by the French. The small percentage of English-speaking people were exiled Tories from the American Revolution. Arriving less than a year before the onset of hostilities, he recognized that a defense of Canada had to rely on the people who lived there. Prévost strengthened his relationship with the Catholic clergy and with the assembly. These moves were enough to align French Canadian citizens with the British if war came. Canadian militia units were called up and organized: Fencibles, Voltigeurs, Select Embodied Militia, Chasseurs and even one infantry unit of Scotsmen. Months before relations with the Americans broke down, almost four thousand Canadians committed to militia duty.

Prévost's attempts to curry favor with the locals is an indication of just how weak his position was. The governor general filled the dual roles of political leader and military commander. Prévost didn't have many English forces to command. The last time there had been any hostilities in the region had been at the end of the Revolution. Canada was a far-off colony, and England had cut back its military presence to a few thousand men. When tensions flared in the final months of 1811 and simmered into early 1812, a small number of reinforcements were sent in April. Prévost still only had about four thousand Englishmen to defend the entire border. Much of the military infrastructure of the region had been constructed decades ago. British Canada was ill prepared for war, and the governor general, if war came, settled on fighting a prolonged holding action until reinforcements arrived from the other side of the Atlantic. With Europe embroiled in the Napoleonic Wars, it could be a long wait.

The Americans knew this. The United States believed it would be able to subdue Canada with relative ease. During the embargo period, New York reorganized its militia forces. There was a small encampment of regular army in Burlington, Vermont, which became an anchor of military activity. While outdated and neglected, the Crown Point and Ticonderoga installations could be updated if necessary.

The larger picture gives a better glimpse of the size of the American advantage. There was never any overarching belief that the English forces in Canada were enough to move south and conquer any territory. Conversely, months before the war began, U.S. leadership was hatching schemes of moving into Canada with multiple invasions at different locations, something the smaller Canadian and English forces would not be able to cope with. Like a heavyweight fighter who is larger and bulkier than the opposition, the United States believed it could easily push smaller enemy units out of the way. From Detroit, Michigan, all along the Great Lakes and the St. Lawrence, to the Richelieu River and Lake Champlain, regional aggressors had the chance to take Canada and prevent any serious reinforcement from England. Even the vast border with Maine, which had served as an American invasion route during the Revolutionary War, was a possible striking point north.

Quebec City was far enough removed from the border and major American population centers that it was not a defensive concern. Montreal, Canada's other major city in the region, was a different story. American efforts to subjugate Canadian territory northeast of Detroit and the Great Lakes would put pressure all along the St. Lawrence River. If the Americans were able to attack from Lake Erie, it was a quick sail to Montreal. Its distance from the American border made it vulnerable. It was obvious American forces would mass somewhere in New York or New England. In this region specific to the Champlain Valley and the Richelieu River corridor, the Canadian militia and English army units were at a considerable disadvantage. The Richelieu River made any defense of Montreal difficult. Only a generation prior, during the onset of the American Revolution, American forces had been able to sail north on Lake Champlain and occupy Montreal—they came close to seizing Quebec City. The Richelieu River was key to any defense south of Montreal. With Montreal so exposed, it would be like starting a chess game with the king in check. It was not checkmate, but it wasn't the position the English or Canadians wanted to be in.

As the early months of 1812 elapsed, the U.S. Congress funded preparations for war. The army sent Colonel Isaac Clark of the Eleventh Infantry to Burlington to begin preparations for the conflict. Clark purchased land in Burlington that would be used as a staging area later in the war and organized recruitment centers in select communities.

An in-depth review of the English and Canadian forces just north of Lake Champlain reveals just how difficult a situation Prévost was in. Geographically, the Americans controlled Lake Champlain. Vermont lay to the east and New York to the west. Their northern borders are an east–west line less than a mile north of the forty-fifth parallel. The uppermost portion of the lake, perhaps no more than a few hundred feet, is in Canadian waters where the larger lake empties into the Richelieu River. With Rouses Point on the New York side and Alburgh on the Vermont side, this is where the Americans had placed their customshouses.

The only other stretch of open water Canada had any claim to was the small northern edge of Missisquoi Bay, just a few miles east of the Richelieu. The area was strategically useless. There were no shipbuilding facilities in Missisquoi Bay. The small River du Sud provided partial access to the land north of Alburgh, but there is no outlet into the bay. The portage of smaller boats, mainly bateaux and canoes, was possible, but their use in Missisquoi Bay meant any Canadian or English vessel had only one outlet to the broader lake: down through American waters. From a military perspective, there was little advantage to putting a shipyard within the bay. The waters near the shore are shallow and only reach a depth of twelve to sixteen feet. It made no sense to make access to Missisquoi Bay a priority.

The obvious choice was for the English to focus on what infrastructure already existed. Initially, Prévost believed the existing defensive framework was outdated and not worth using. His assessment quickly changed.

With the knowledge that much of the conflict would be fought out west at first, Prévost devoted much of his regular army to the Great Lakes region. That left the area south of Montreal pretty bare. Like the Americans, Prévost had to depend on local militia to build his defense. Despite some initial trouble, about 350 Canadian Voltigeurs and a small complement of Indians were commanded by Major Charles de Salaberry and stationed at Chambly.[39] That these men were not stationed directly on the border is an indication of the weakness of the English position. It also is a nod to the English intelligence services, which seemed to have enough knowledge of the American military units to know there wasn't much of an early threat in the Lake Champlain region. They knew the threat would be emerging; it just wasn't there at the start of the war.

Some of that intelligence came from travelers moving through the border. Others had more discreet ways of moving information. Some sources lived on the American side of the border and passed information north. An example would be Francis Duclos of Sheldon, Vermont. In 1812, Duclos sent intelligence that, while there were plenty of Vermonters against the prospect of hostilities, the national attitude favored an invasion of Canada. Duclos slipped information to England throughout the war.[40]

The British made various efforts to strengthen their ability to wage a defensive campaign. An old blockhouse at Lacolle Mill, originally built near

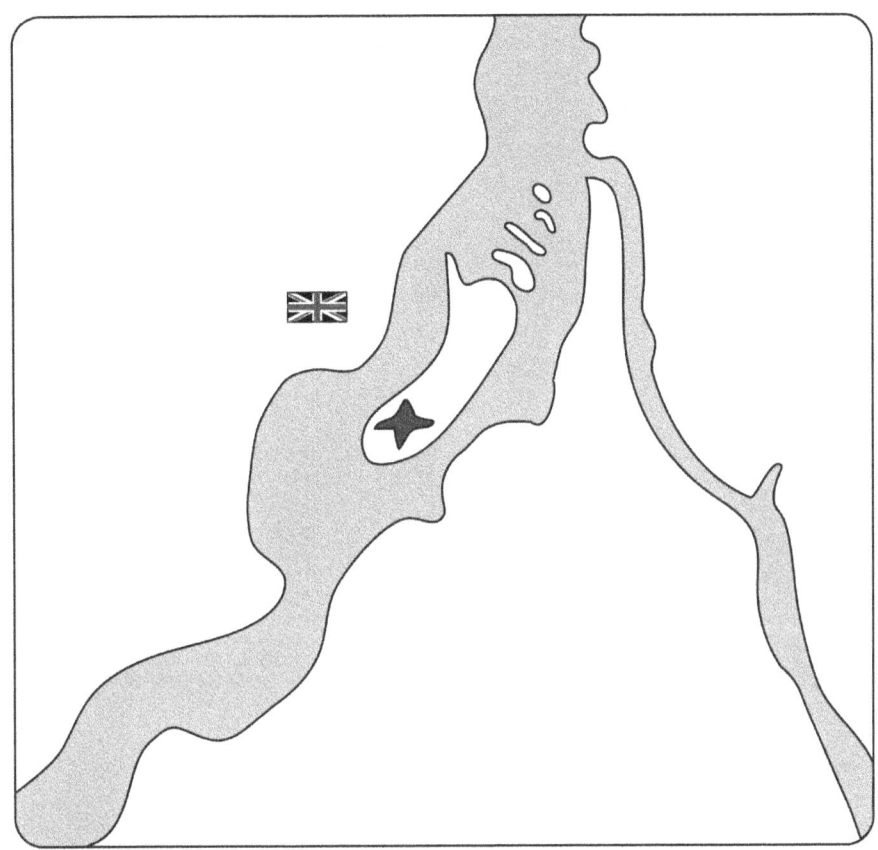

The English base at Isle Aux Noix. As the crow flies, it is about a dozen miles from Swanton. *Artwork by Lindsay DiDio.*

the end of the Revolutionary War, was repaired and updated. Ash Island, at the very southern tributary of the Richelieu, a very small and otherwise insignificant piece of property, was examined for use as an advanced post. At the onset of war, barracks were constructed at Burtonville, just west of Isle Aux Noix on the Richelieu, to support any future troop assignments. Reserve units were held farther north, in the area southeast of Montreal.[41] Perhaps because of their experience with invasions during the French and Indian War and American Revolution, the initial assessment was that Isle Aux Noix was not a particularly defendable position. That assessment would quickly change.

On the doorstep of war, even though they would be the regional aggressors, the Americans also were ill prepared. There was already a small military presence in Burlington, and American leaders started to assess the value of Plattsburgh, New York. On the east side of the lake, Swanton was a natural location to increase the American military presence. The town already had links to the federal government. Jabez Penniman had lived there while directing the efforts of the *Fly* and *Lark* in the period before the war.[42] The sloop *Juno* had made supply runs between the northeast corner of the lake, Alburgh and Burlington. Swanton had already hosted smaller numbers of federal units in the effort to clamp down on smuggling. Swanton's importance was, of course, linked to the larger military assets in the theater, but its role has been historically understated.

Colonel Isaac Clark of the Eleventh Infantry Regiment arrived in Burlington just weeks before the conflict. He took command of the small number of regulars already stationed there, prepared the New York side of the lake and engaged in the unpopular task of preparing Vermont for war. One of his early accomplishments was to negotiate the purchase of two five-acre plots of land on the waterfront in Burlington. As the spring faded away and the long days of summer approached, work began on a large cantonment to house future units destined for the area.[43] Valentine Goodrich, also of the Eleventh Infantry and a Swanton native, received orders to set up a recruitment station in that town.[44] Other recruitment centers were set up in Burlington, Middlebury and Montpelier. In May, Governor Jonas Galusha issued orders for the militia to start working in conjunction with the growing U.S. military presence.

These preparations coincided with the completion of the cantonment in Swanton that would house militia or federal soldiers patrolling along the frontier. Any unit ordered to block smuggling activity from Alburgh to Richford would be housed in Swanton. With the real possibility of war arriving, the project was likely expanded to provide a base of operations near the border. The barracks were constructed from the pine forest within walking distance of the Missisquoi River and located on the village green. Most of the village lay along the river. The barracks was situated on the highest land opposite the village, just east of the green, but a few rods west of a small stream in town. The site featured three buildings in the shape of a crescent with a large parade ground between the structures and the village.[45] A hospital was part of the cantonment there.

Valentine Goodrich's early role in the prewar weeks had to have been exceedingly difficult. Northern Franklin County, Vermont, had already been a hotbed of smuggling for at least five years, since the onset of the embargo. To some locals, the completion of such large military structures was a welcome sight. The townspeople of Swanton would not have known about the weakness of the enemy forces near Montreal. They heard rumors and read the newspaper accounts of building tensions. To others, the growing military presence felt like a military occupation. Those whose livelihood depended on trade with larger markets had never supported the embargo in the first place. To them, the embargo, the *Black Snake* affair and all the smuggling over the last decade was a cause-and-effect relationship. The idea of hostilities with neighbors to the north was foreign and detestable. Valentine Goodrich, Isaac Clark, the newly constructed barracks, squads of the Eleventh Infantry, elements of the militia sent to the area…they were all part of the problem, instruments of government preventing natural commerce that would feed families, pay bills and eliminate debts.

Goodrich reported to Clark on June 5, from Swanton, that his efforts were going well enough. There was some opposition from members of the Federalist Party, but he communicated that he'd opened the recruitment station in town on June 2. Five "good able fellows" had already enlisted with him, and there were a number of interested new recruits. Goodrich was getting interest from men with families and asked Colonel Clark about the appropriateness of wives receiving government rations.[46]

War was declared on June 18, 1812.

4
SWANTON, A COG IN THE WAR MACHINE

Summer 1812

News of the outbreak of war did not reach the north country for nine days. Swanton's 1,700 residents were no longer just part of a border community, they were the northernmost outpost along Lake Champlain. The cantonment in town was no longer just a place for the militia and a few federal agents and the U.S. army to train, recruit and patrol the border. It was now a real military installation six miles from enemy territory. The elderly of the community knew their history; they recalled Lake Champlain's importance during earlier conflicts. Swanton's geographic location meant that even if it wasn't going to be directly involved, some of the townspeople would play a role in the coming conflict. Husbands and fathers in their twenties, thirties and forties had to be thinking about militia service. There was the real possibility of combat with enemy forces. Wives and mothers wondered if they would become widows.

The feelings ran even deeper than that. Based on the amount of the illegal activity that defined local commerce for years, portions of the population were forced to reconsider their individual roles in trade with the north. It was no longer about just making a profit. The arguments that one had to feed a family or the government had no business limiting commerce changed with the declaration of war. Anyone making a profit from getting potash or timber over the border prior to June 18, 1812, may have had an intellectually defendable position. Prior to the declaration of war, it was illegal activity. Now it was treasonous behavior.

The move from peace to war did change a lot of things for a lot of people, however. While the numbers were initially quite small, U.S. soldiers were in Swanton and nearby towns every day. Any rumor about British military activity became a potential threat. Locking one's doors at night against thieves or thugs didn't matter when measured against the threat of invasion. The residents of Franklin County were justifiably scared.

Vermont governor Jonas Galusha called out the militia and ordered the First Regiment under Colonel William Williams to assemble in Swanton. The typical duties of observing the border were expanded to actual military drilling and patrolling for enemy units coming from Canada. Fear seized the towns along the Quebec border. The selectmen from Richford, just eighteen miles from Swanton and situated on the Canadian border, wrote Clark in late June asking that militia and arms be sent to their community.[47] Selectmen William Rogers, Levi Grout, Asa Morris, Bradford Powell, Stephen Carpenter, Caleb Roy and one other wanted fifty troops with the appropriate weaponry sent to their township. The official request went to Governor Galusha as well. Clark, attempting to deal with heavy antiwar sentiment, organized his own forces in Burlington and began a buildup of troops in Plattsburgh. He also tried to reach the public by publishing his thoughts in the *Burlington Sentinel*.[48] His message was meant for all Vermonters, but he went out of his way to address the fears of the people living along the border. Clark, while preparing the area for armed conflict, attempted to persuade Vermonters that Canadian citizens did not want to make war on the people of the United States. He stated that the real enemy were the tyrants leading the enemy military, representatives of the British Crown.

The colonel's published remarks may have been seen as somewhat dismissive of the concerns of the northern communities, but his thinking may have been colored by discussions of a flag of truce only weeks into the conflict. It was not uncommon for accounts in the press to be picked up by newspapers on both sides of the border. Clark's wording supports this idea, as he pointed out the "iron hands of the Governor" that never consults with the Canadian people.

Although Clark's words in print were meant to calm fears, the military buildup was beginning to gain steam. On July 16, the local newspapers reported that militia units mustered in Montpelier, while U.S. Army recruits gathered at the recruitment center there and traveled to Burlington.

The U.S. leadership wanted to invade Canada. When measuring the size of the fighting forces and the potential for invasion, any Englishman or French Canadian had much more reason to be concerned than anyone living in Swanton, Richford or Derby.

There were reasons why the United States thought it could march troops into Canada relatively easily. Prévost's attention was by necessity all over the map, but intelligence he received told him the Americans were not yet ready along the Lake Champlain corridor. His preparations to organize the local militia proved insightful after the United States declared war. Prévost heard the news about the declaration of war at about the same time that word spread in northern Vermont. He called up the Canadian militia in the last days of June and issued orders to prepare for a defense of the Richelieu River area.[49]

South of the border, it is not clear when the first companies of Williams's regiment arrived in Swanton, but by early August there were more than four hundred soldiers stationed in town.[50] As they took up their assignments, the chance for peace was not abandoned. Colonel Baynes, a representative of the English government, came from Canada to meet with American generals in upstate New York. A brief truce for the theater was arranged. Baynes was Prévost's representative, and there was a sliver of hope war might be averted.

In Swanton, the companies of Williams's unit had arrived and were drilling, training and starting to patrol. No known document has been discovered that gives specific details on the size of the barracks. Approximately one-third of the men would have bunked in each building, indicating each structure was likely in the range of two hundred feet long and more than fifteen to twenty feet wide.[51]

Williams's regiment was made up of eleven companies, but there is some evidence only eight of them reported to Swanton. A company is a medium-sized military unit, usually composed of anywhere from forty to seventy-five men. The companies commanded by Phelps, Pettis, Taylor, Saxe, Kendall and Barnes are mentioned in the *Swanton Town History* as serving in the late summer and fall of 1812. It is not entirely clear if the missing companies were Lowry's, Wilson's, Dorrance's or Robbins's, which were the remaining companies under Williams's command. These units may not have been stationed along with the other companies. Oliver Lowry's company of approximately seventy was from Richmond and the surrounding towns but does not appear to have been deployed in Swanton.[52] The same goes for John Robbins's company from mostly Addison County. Put together from the towns of Shoreham, Whiting, Bridport, Panton, Addison and Cornwall, their enlistment records indicate they were called up from July

9 to December 8, four months and twenty-nine days of service. Joseph Dorrance's fifty-man company had about the same enlistment period. Boswell Wilson's forty-five-man company was called up, but there is no direct evidence of service in Swanton, either. References from the town's history book about Asa Scoville's Rifle Company, as well as a company of cavalry being in the area in the fall of 1812, are probably incorrect, although both show up later in the war. It is also not clear if all the units were in town together, as manpower was needed to patrol all along the frontier. Some units would have been required to maintain supply lines.

Two months beyond the declaration of war, the local military commanders entertained the idea of a negotiated peace. In early August, American generals based in Albany, New York, agreed to host Colonel Baynes, Prévost's attempt at an olive branch. The British wanted to avoid the commencement of hostilities so close to Montreal. Baynes's path brought him down from Montreal, into upstate New York, on to Lake Champlain and down to Albany by boat. Ultimately the American political leadership rejected the truce. Baynes's path back to Canada brought him back to Lake Champlain, up to Burlington and overland to Swanton.[53] The return trip to Quebec took him through the growing encampment in Swanton.[54] American leadership warned Isaac Clark that Baynes was being escorted through his area, and despite the effort at a truce, American generals described Baynes as a spy.

Even though action had not started in the Champlain Valley, open fighting was underway in the West. News coverage of the war was available in both larger national papers and smaller local ones, and details of the failed American invasion around Detroit filtered into the Northeast. What was expected to be the advance of a grand army had turned into a major victory for the English and Canadians. In Vermont, New York and Quebec, the weather was still temperate enough to support an invasion of Canada by U.S. forces, but the clock was starting to tick.

That mobilization was going slowly. The arrival of units depended on a wide range of issues. When towns got the statewide order to muster, how quickly each company was able to organize depended on the occupations of those called to duty, the distance they needed to march or sail to get to Swanton, the local weather conditions and the condition of the roads.

Rumors of enemy troop strength just miles to the north appeared in press accounts, giving citizens a scare during August. Some newspapers and citizens spread information that the British were on the move, that English soldiers were already on the march. While there undoubtably were patrols, the fear was probably stoked by observations of the Canadian militia preparing defensive measures against an American incursion. There appears to have been verifiable intelligence about an English regiment at St. Jean, but any other stories about an imminent British invasion were false.[55] At this stage, the British did not have the manpower.

Based on *Rosters of the War 1812–14*, it appears that seven of the companies in Williams's regiment had assembled in Swanton by early August. Stephen Pettis commanded about seventy-two men from Grand Isle County and other communities along the lake. Those coming from the islands needed to boat to Swanton, as there were no bridges at the time. They had departed their local communities by July 22 and probably arrived within a few days. Their enlistments were set to run out on December 9. Hezekiah Barns's unit was from Charlotte and western Chittenden County. His sixty-seven men had enlistments for four months and twenty-odd days. Many of the men from George Kendall's company came from the towns in eastern Franklin County, less than a day's march from their destination. James Taylor's fifty-six militiamen came from southern Franklin County and some communities in Lamoille County. Matthew Phelps was from New Haven. He and his sixty men arrived and started to serve but, as the war buildup unfolded through the fall, received specific orders for a unique task. It is possible that either Dorrance's, Lowry's or Robbins's men were moved to the border to maintain numbers on the line. Based on the length of enlistments, the last unit to arrive in Swanton was Conrade Saxe of Highgate, his men not being mustered until September 1.[56] The inclusion of nearly eighty men from the town directly on the Canadian border only meant trouble. Some of the men from the *Black Snake* affair had direct links to Highgate, and the smuggling in the area continued. The shores of Missisquoi Bay form a cup along both towns, and from there Canada is close enough to see. As described earlier, it had been nearly impossible for revenue cutters to control those waters in the years before the outbreak of war. Highgate, with several small back roads leading into Quebec, had been a safe land route for lawbreakers. The inclusion of Saxe's men into Williams's regiment may have been a smart move on paper, considering the men knew the territory, but events would soon lead to doubts about their loyalties. It would be a major headache for all involved.

Regardless, young men always need jobs, and in wartime, the military is hiring. Swanton's recruitment center was proving productive for Isaac Clark and the U.S. Army. Lieutenant Goodrich busily filled out the muster role for the company he would command as part of the Eleventh Infantry

View of Missisquoi Bay looking south. *Photo by Armand Messier of northernvermontaerial.com.*

View of Missisquoi Bay looking north. The land and the lake were a hotbed of smuggling activity. *Photo by Armand Messier of northernvermontaerial.com.*

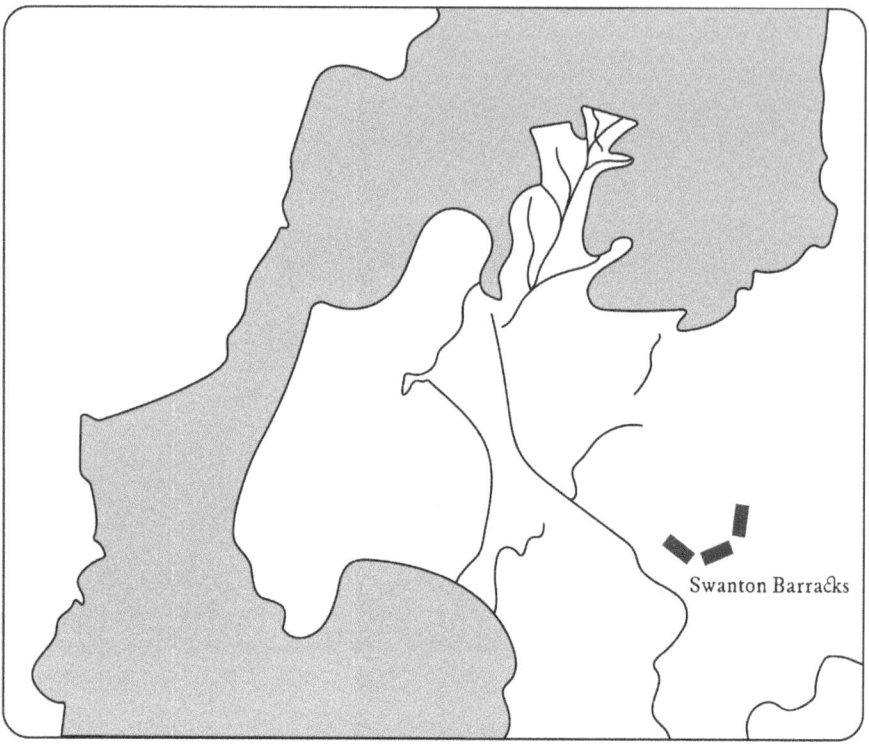

The location of the Swanton Barracks. *Artwork by Lindsay DiDio.*

Regiment. As summer slipped away, about 17 percent of the men enlisted in his company had done so in Swanton.

Almost two months into the war, and the flag of truce a thing of the past, the last weeks of August were critical for both sides. The Americans were trying to bring enough forces up to mount an invasion, the British doing what they could to blunt that effort. Colonel Clark worked to have the plots at the Burlington waterfront turned into a camp for soldiers entering the area. His men set about turning those ten acres into a full-fledged military base.

As early as late August, the Americans started to control Lake Champlain. Any invasion of Canada depended on domination of the lake. If the British had any foothold, they could harass supply lines, hit infantrymen packed in bateaux being transported from Burlington to Plattsburgh and strike deep into American territory. There was no question on the American side: If they did not have the lake, there would be no invasion of Canada.

The growing encampment in Plattsburgh started to become notable by late August. There were at least three companies of Colonel Clark's Eleventh Regiment in upstate New York by September 4.[57] The organization and infrastructure needed to transport that many men and their supplies was also in place by early September. The U.S. government embraced a significant effort to assemble plenty of bateaux that could transport their forces up and down the lake. Bateaux were the preferred method of transport during wartime and became multidimensional. Some were fitted with a small mast and, with the appropriate rigging, could take advantage of gusty winds for quick movement. Others were simply equipped with oars, and the soldiers packed into them had to row from one location to another. Some were constructed for possible combat, with small three-pound cannons fitted at their bows. The U.S. military contracted to have 160 built, and by late August many were already in use. They were approximately thirty-seven feet long and eight feet wide and carried approximately forty soldiers each. The bateaux were constructed at Whitehall, New York, near the southern region of the lake. The importance of this early effort cannot be understated, as it put the Americans one step ahead of the enemy. With American forces stationed in Swanton, Plattsburgh and Burlington, and the defensive blockhouses and batteries in place near the border for the start of the war, troop movements would be unencumbered. The British would not have the chance to seize the advantage. The bateaux initiative was successful enough that another 60 or so were ordered.[58] During the brief Baynes armistice, the Colonel witnessed some of the boats already in service and, upon his return to Canada, reported their use back to his command.[59]

In past military activity on the lake, the side with the larger vessels had a distinct advantage. This had proven true during the French and Indian Wars and the Revolution. While the Americans were investing in their bateaux, they also knew they had to think bigger. Lieutenant Sidney Smith, essentially the early naval commander on the lake, attained control of the two gunboats that had been built in 1809 and had been used to confront smugglers. Slightly larger than the bateaux, these were brought to Plattsburgh, and Smith began repairing and arming them. While built as gunboats, their identification and service would effectively designate them as scows for much of the war.[60]

Gunboats, scows and bateaux would not be enough, though. Based on the fleets the British fielded in 1777 and 1778, the military knew it had to think in larger terms. At some point in August, the rights to a number of commercial and private sloops were obtained, drastically improving the American position. With construction facilities at Whitehall, some degree of naval yards at Burlington and Plattsburgh, the addition of these larger vessels further cemented American control of Champlain. The sloops were sailing vessels with a large single mast. They could be heavily armed with large cannons and still maneuver. At this very early date, they were not armed yet, but that would happen soon enough. The vessels were the *Fox*, *Hunter*, *Jupiter*, *Champlain*, *Juno* and one other sloop.[61] The *Juno* had been used as a supply vessel by the government years before, against the earlier smuggling efforts. Some historical ambiguity exists about the origin of the vessel that became the *President*. One print source at the time suggested it was originally the *Fox*, while some historians speculate it was built during the summer of 1812. The *President* would serve as the early flagship of the American navy. The other sloops would be used as transports until the naval effort was better organized.

During the first week of September, the Sixth and Fifteenth Infantry Regiments left the crowded encampment in Burlington and were brought across Lake Champlain. The Sixth Regiment was commanded by Colonel Simonds. The Fifteenth, which played a significant role in Plattsburgh's part in the War of 1812, was commanded by Colonel Pike. Their arrival coincided with that of General Bloomfield, one of the regional commanders of the war effort.

A sad lesson of war is that not all casualties occur during combat. Perhaps an indication of things to come was the accidental death of Dr. Brewster. He was one of the surgeons for Colonel Clark's Eleventh Regiment. In the first weeks of September, Brewster fell overboard while being transported from Burlington to Plattsburgh. Efforts were made to save him, but the man drowned.[62]

As the last warmth of summer evaporated, military activity was not limited to Swanton or other parts of the Champlain Valley. The northern border of Vermont, along the east and central portion of the state, received attention as well. While isolated, the Northeast Kingdom border stretched for miles with Quebec. With war underway, Vermont decided it needed a military presence in the region as well. Derby, located nearly fifty miles from Lake Champlain, was somewhat strategically located near Lake Memphremagog, a mid-sized body of water that had been used during earlier conflicts. Like Swanton, a barracks was erected to accommodate potential troop movements. The Derby Town Land Records for September

1812 indicate that citizen Timothy Hinman donated property north of Derby Center, just west of Hinman Pond, known today as Lake Derby.[63] The town ledger indicates W. Childs was paid for work on barns or buildings next to the water, to provision the troops. Captain Rufus Stewart of the local militia probably oversaw the modifications to the buildings and the updates to the property. Based on the number of adult male citizens available for militia duty, the size of cantonment was small. One estimate had the capacity at no more than sixty or so men, with only a third of that number being housed overnight.[64] The exact location is not known, but it is believed there were barracks, officers' quarters, a guardhouse and possibly a supply depot.[65] Much of this work was started in August, at about the same time that militia units reported to Burlington and Swanton. The first soldiers to man the Derby outpost were from that town and the neighboring communities of Holland and Morgan. It was a couple of days' march from the main activity near Lake Champlain and small enough to avoid notice by major British military units or Canadian militia. However, the intensity of the smuggling along the border reinforced the need for an American military presence. The Quebec town north of the line, Stanstead, was populated by people like their American neighbors. Trade and commerce had existed for a generation, and the declaration of war was not enough to stop them. The main purpose of the Derby post was to cut down on the amount of cattle being driven over the line.[66]

By September, the drums of war were beating in the Champlain Valley. Generals Bloomfield and Dearborn were under pressure to commence an invasion of Quebec, with Montreal being the primary objective. The military presence in the area increased greatly, with regular army units arriving in Plattsburgh and Burlington at an accelerated pace.

With Canadian forces collecting in the area, the realities of supply and demand increased in the need for American products north of the border. If it was a hot spot for smuggling before, it did not take long for the scale of the illegal trade to expand. On September 17, a writer in one of the local papers publicly accused some of the men on duty in Swanton of participating in the smuggling activities.[67] Concerns were raised about the militiamen associated with Conrade Saxe's company from Highgate. It was almost too easy for individuals to have their loyalties compromised when they had already been trading with Canada for years before militia service. They had valuable knowledge of paths in the woods and local patrols and already knew people willing to trade with Canadians. Swanton's long shoreline in Missisquoi Bay provided a tempting view of

Quebec. Highgate also has shoreline along the Missisquoi, and its portion of the border with Canada is nearly six miles long. If Vermonters heard stories of militiamen participating in the smuggling, the men of Saxe's unit were prime suspects. The problem wasn't just the men from Swanton or Highgate. As the prewar years demonstrated, efforts to clamp down on the black market were just doomed to fail. And while men from Swanton and Highgate come under the historical microscope during the first months of the conflict, blame likely lies all along the chain of command for the militia. The First Regiment under Colonel Williams was also made up of men from Grand Isle County and from other frontier towns like Enosburgh and Richford. Colonel Williams, headquartered in Swanton, was up against an impossible task.

While attempting to deal with the public fallout, Colonel Williams sent his own letter to the Burlington papers, and they published it on September 19. He confronted the accusations and demanded the writer of the charges come forth with specifics.[68] The situation north of Plattsburgh wasn't much better. Militia units and customs agents were having difficulty cutting down on the illegal activity there.[69]

Despite this, the military build-up was well under way. In addition to Williams's regiment being stationed in Swanton, three others were mustered. Colonel Jonathan Williams and Colonel Stephen Martindale both commanded full regiments that received orders to cross the lake. Additionally, Colonel Edward Fifield was ordered to Swanton with his

View of Missisquoi Bay looking into Canada. Vermonters wondered about the enemy military forces to the north early in the war. *Photo by Armand Messier of northernvermontaerial.com.*

View of Missisquoi Bay looking into Swanton and Highgate. *Photo by Armand Messier of northernvermontaerial.com.*

regiment, adding another nine companies to the growing contingent in the northwest portion of the state.[70] Like the companies before them, the arriving units settled into Swanton as they arrived. The first was Andrew Dodge's company from the Hartland area, whose enlistments and arrival in Swanton likely happened shortly after September 5.[71] Next was Enos Walker's company.[72] As the last weeks of September approached, the rest of the companies, including Wheatley, Wheeler, Mason, Durkee, Morrill, Taylor and Rogers, arrived for their border duties.[73] Elements of Mason's company received orders to patrol the area in the Northeast Kingdom and were stationed at barracks in Derby.[74] Not all of Fifield's companies were in Swanton at the same time, as some press accounts reported Swanton still had the original four hundred servicemen as September bled into October.[75] That would change. Men from both sides were approaching the border, and tensions continued to mount.

Among the inaccurately reported threats along the frontier were the stories of English-organized Indian war parties massing to the north.[76] By mid-September, both Plattsburgh and Burlington newspapers reported hundreds of hostile Indians massing at "St. Armand, Isle Aux Noix and Odelltown."[77] By this point of early fall, the old English naval

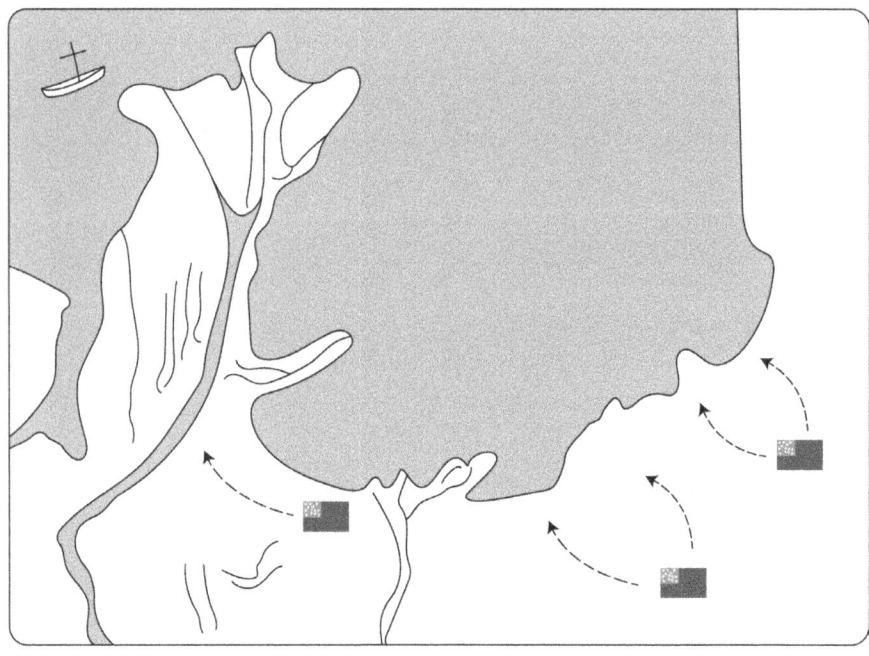

The Vermont militia assembles in Swanton. An early militia flag was used to make the distinction between militia units and U.S. Army units. *Artwork by Lindsay DiDio.*

base at Isle Aux Noix was finally being reevaluated. Near the southern tip of the Richelieu River, it simply couldn't continue to be neglected. Oldelltown is just over the border from upstate New York. St. Armand is the Canadian community north of Highgate, Vermont. As the crow flies, each is less than a day's march away from Swanton. While the actual extent of the Indian threat could not have been known at the time, anyone old enough to remember the Revolution certainly recalled Indian raids as part of Burgoyne's 1777 invasion or stories of the raids during the French and Indian War. The rumors of massing natives put the militiamen in Swanton on alert.

Around the third week of September, the Plattsburgh and Burlington papers reported on the size of the British naval force at Isle Aux Noix. The press accounts of two gunboats, several row galleys and an unknown number of bateaux were not welcome news. There was one printed account that the British had already moved five gunboats to the island, but this was an exaggeration. Historical records indicate that once the British realized the Americans had a sizable naval presence on the lake, they moved assets to the area. It was reported in late September that along with the roving bands of Indians, the British may have had as many as 450 soldiers at Isle Aux Noix. This number was close to accurate, but the majority of those men would have had little or no offensive purpose. The island was an out of date, neglected, and old installation. While three months had passed, the soldiers stationed there had plenty to handle without thinking about launching raids into Vermont or New York. The effort north of the border was largely defensive in nature. While overstated, the American anxiety about invasion was not without merit. The short distance between the Richelieu River and Missisquoi Bay would have provided an ambitious raiding party a chance to strike after a brief portage. Roads supporting such an effort on the Canadian side of the bay were well known to the locals.[78]

It should be noted that the British naval resources devoted to Isle Aux Noix would have been used to defend territory rather than launch offensive actions. The American press account of five gunboats appears to be incorrect, as the British moved two gunboats from Montreal, likely in late August, and then a third at some point prior to the fall. Prévost realized they would be useful along the border and sailed them from Montreal to the Richelieu. The gunboats were the *Beresford*, which was forty-five feet long and eleven feet, six inches wide, and the *Brock* and *Popham*, each slightly smaller and differently designed. The two smaller vessels measured approximately forty-four feet long and eleven feet wide.[79]

The activity of infantry assigned to the island would have been primarily to keep an eye on American activity to the south. Prévost expected the Americans would attack, and they would not be able to bypass a full military installation so close to the border. Isle Aux Noix and any surrounding defensive arrangements would have to be taken out during an American invasion.

The British officers and engineers quickly went about restoring the defensive positions. Redoubts, or small defendable positions, were restored on the western and southern ends of the island. These were fitted with cannons meant to harass any force moving up from the south or along the Richelieu River. Smaller defensive emplacements were constructed on the shores opposite either side of the island. The most significant effort was put into restoring the old fort, which lay north from the redoubts. The fort protected the shipyard, which was expanded and enlarged.[80] This was in concert with upgrading the defensive works at Lacolle Mills, earlier in the fall, and the work on Ash Island, at the mouth of Richelieu. It was just an attempt to hold on until more powerful forces could be brought to bear. However, any American living on the border saw a growing enemy presence only miles away.

Additionally, the Canadian militia in the communities along the border were called to duty. Prévost rightly saw the need to develop his defenses in the region and knew he had to rely on the local militia to supplement his weak forces. To at least anchor the defense to the east of the Richelieu, multiple companies were mustered. Seven were mustered from Stanstead, four in Hatley and three were brought into service from Barnston. Infantry generally needs the support of cavalry, so a company of horsemen was also brought in to serve that region.[81]

5

THERE AND BACK AGAIN

FALL 1812

The activity in Swanton and northwestern Vermont comes further into focus as the anticipated American invasion inched closer. It was the primary location for the American government to once again try to clamp down on smuggling. Any hope that the declaration of war and the mobilization against England would spread patriotic feelings or bring opportunists to heel quickly faded, especially when the militiamen themselves were under suspicion. As American general Joseph Bloomfield gathered his forces in Plattsburgh, the most likely invasion route became obvious. The grand plan was for the army to leave upstate New York, quash any opposition and be in Montreal before Christmas. U.S. Army regulars poured across the lake from Burlington, and the size of the overall force increased. Swanton provided an interesting opportunity to keep the enemy off balance. Within striking distance of the enemy, any American presence there became a possible invasion route. Finally, with all the naval activity in the waters of Lake Champlain, the military needed to find the appropriate men to man the vessels. Swanton provided that opportunity.

Valentine Goodrich received orders from General Bloomfield in September and October that men from the units in Swanton were needed to man the vessels being fitted for service on Lake Champlain.[82] Operation of the sixty-one-foot sloop *Hunter* was given to the men of Valentine Goodrich's company of the Eleventh Regiment. Many of their enlistment records specifically state service onboard the sloops of Lake Champlain.[83] Unfortunately, history did not record all of them. John Lamphiere, who enlisted in Swanton in the early weeks of the war, was "detailed for Flotilla." Nicholas Frimmer's military paperwork has him "on board of the Navy." Rufus Austin was designated to be "on board Sloop of War." The exact date of when this personnel transfer occurred was never recorded but historically aligns with the need to fill out the complements of the larger vessels on the lake. However, it wasn't just Goodrich's company that would be called upon. Perhaps because of Valentine Goodrich's assessment of specific militia captains and companies serving in northwest Vermont, elements of the Vermont militia were mined as well. To fill out the complement and crew of the sixty-five-foot *President*, the largest of the American vessels, orders were given to Phelps's company of Williams's regiment who had been in Swanton for several weeks. The other companies of Williams's regiment received no such orders and remained along the frontier. Matthew Phelps and his eighty-man company had been in Swanton since August, but now operated naval vessels on the most important waterway in the theater. They were responsible for cutting down on smuggling, running the transportation system for the army gathering in upstate New York and confronting any English ships that strayed south.

The orders for Swanton units to crew the boats loosely coincided with the arrival of Thomas MacDonough to the theater. MacDonough was a navy man, not from the army, and initially he had issues working his way into the already existing command structure that had developed on both sides of the lake.[84] McDonough arrived around October 8 in Burlington and communicated with General Dearborn shortly afterward. He would eventually take the *President* as his flagship during a good portion of the war, but at this early juncture it was the only one of the sloops the army refused to relinquish. By early October, the navy was arming the sloops in Whitehall, New York. Lieutenant Sidney Smith, who had worked on one of the gunboats in the first attempts to get some semblance of the navy going, probably helped with the armaments being set in the southern portion of the lake. One detailed account of the naval activity is the journal of Captain John Scott of the Fifteenth Infantry Regiment. Scott's unit marched from points south and west before they reached the southern areas of Lake Champlain. Scott, writing letters in late September and early October, notes there were eight sloops in operation at that point in time.[85] His counting of eight sloops at this juncture is evidence that the navy had transferred the gunboats or scows south, and Scott likely included them in his count.

Looking at events with a wider lens, there were supposed to be the three invasions of Canada, the success of each individual thrust designed to put more and more pressure on Prévost and his outnumbered forces. The first indication things were falling apart was the American defeat at Detroit. The second prong of the invasion took shape along the Niagara frontier about the same time as units were getting organized in Plattsburgh, Swanton and Burlington. In the first week of October, American commanders made plans to cross the Niagara River and take British Queenston, the main community in the area. From there, the Americans wanted to move along the St. Lawrence and threaten Montreal from the southwest. Once again, what had been drawn up on paper failed miserably in the field. At Queenston Heights, the Americans pushed forward with only about 20 percent of their available fighting force and then British reserves reached the battlefield. It was a defeat for the American invasion force in more ways than one. Perhaps foreshadowing more unpleasantness for the Champlain Valley route, militia units from Pennsylvania and New York, who had assembled and trained with the U.S. Army prior to the Niagara invasion, refused to cross the border. American casualties were high, and by the second week of October the grand plan to knock the British out of the war early was crumbling. There was still one major opportunity along Lake Champlain, but time was running out.

Even as things started to come together for the eventual push northward, Generals Bloomfield and Dearborn knew their window of opportunity was closing. While summer and early fall provide prime fighting conditions, late fall and winter do not. In summer, the ground is dry, and movement of war parties can be camouflaged by full leaf cover. Warmer weather is not as hard on equipment. The nights had gotten colder in September. The arrival of October brought reds, browns and golds to the foliage. Due to the approach of winter, seasonal difficulties started to occur as the leaves began to fall. Soon any push north would be restricted by snow, ice or inhospitably cold temperatures.

The weather in the late months of 1812 was wet.[86] With soldiers exposed to unsanitary conditions and the arrival of cold, constant rain showers, various diseases started to spread within the camps and affected the total number of soldiers available for duty. While units started to prepare for the invasion of southern Quebec, doctors contended with sick and dying soldiers. There were constant rain showers and even a few snow flurries after October 10.[87] Dr. Charles Mann, who recorded the spread of the diseases, recognized the role the poor weather played.[88] He wrote that it was very cold, with earlier than normal frosts. Despite this, American leadership knew army camp life brought with it some level of sickness, and plans commenced for the trek north. However, as the weeks passed, more and more soldiers were too ill to join the campaign.

By early October, the bulk of the Vermont militia was mustering to be a part of the army gathering around Plattsburgh. Most of them gathered in Burlington; the fleet of bateaux and the hastily refitted sloops and scows brought them across the lake. Martindale's regiment, consisting of about ten companies, crossed the lake in the second week of October. By Wednesday the thirteenth, most of his men were camped just north of Plattsburgh.[89] The company commanders in this regiment were Wright, Strait, Hopkins, Ormsbee, Needham, Hotchkiss, Scoville, Brown, Cross and Richardson.

Jonathan Williams's regiment, comprising another nine companies, arrived on Sunday, October 17. The company commanders were Sabin, Adams, Bingham, Briggs, Parson, Preston, Noyce, Phelps and Burnap. As events of the fall unfolded, some of the company commanders would later be linked with the barracks in Swanton. Martindale sketched a map of the Plattsburgh military activity on October 20.[90] The Vermont militia regiments were encamped along Plattsburgh Bay and the Saranac River. It was the farthest any unit would be from any fighting if Plattsburgh were raided by English and Canadian units coming down from Isle Aux Noix. It happened to be "in the rear" relative to the rest of the encamped units and the Canadian Border.

Another boat-related accident occurred during October, this time with no fatalities. Men working the vessels from Phelps's company, originally stationed in Swanton, now sailing the sloops, were involved in the mishap. They were operating the cannons on one of the vessels in a ceremony to note the arrival of General Bloomfield, who was doing an inspection. Peter Bradley fired one of the cannons and was caught in the recoil. His back was severely injured.[91] Fellow militiamen Cobb Hall and Paul Holly were part of the group that witnessed the accident. Bradley was brought to the shore and received medical attention, but his injuries would hinder him for the rest of his life. Sidney Smith temporarily commanded the vessel.

Back in Swanton, Edward Fifield and William Williams had plenty of smugglers to try to track down. Hiram Mason's unit was stationed along the Derby border and intervened in an effort to sneak beef cattle into southern Quebec.[92] Other units intercepted smugglers in Richford and Berkshire.[93] They were involved in a cat-and-mouse game along back roads and old paths.

American commanders who originally believed an invasion of Quebec would be easy were now waffling on even making a thrust north of Lake

Champlain. Thomas Jefferson had once written, "The acquisition of Canada this year, as far as the neighborhood of Quebec, will be a mere matter of marching."[94] The first months of the war quelled American arrogance, and the situation on the ground in Vermont and New York put doubt on another push north.

Infantry captain John Scott's letters give precise and important information about serving in the region. In one letter during the build-up, he provides specific details of what the men were hearing about enemy forces to the north. Scott, unfamiliar with the territory, documented how far his men would have to travel in the coming cold. Falling prey to the fog of war with everyone else stationed in Plattsburgh, Scott wrote there were close to "1000 Indians at or near the lines," with "1200 regular troops at Isle Aux Noix."

In another letter written on October 28, Scott detailed a conversation he had with some of the leadership and wrote about the size and makeup of the force about to move north.[95] His account from Plattsburgh gives accurate and detailed information about the third prong of the invasion destined for Canada. He estimated there were still over seven hundred militiamen stationed in Vermont. This referenced both Williams's regiment and Colonel Fifield's men in or around Swanton in late October. Some of those men likely served with Colonel Clark's small detachment in Burlington, working on the barracks and buildings along the lake shore. For Swanton, it was a massive military presence. Between the two militia regiments and any of Clark's soldiers in town, the number of soldiers equaled half the civilian population. It paled in comparison with the force assembling in Plattsburgh and was dwarfed by the encampment being prepared in Burlington, but it was a considerable deployment. The horses, men, equipment and supplies stationed along Missisquoi Bay made the area a true military encampment overlooked by contemporary historians.

The anticipated invasion attempt was organized enough where Dearborn and the rest of the American command felt they at least had to try to move north. However, despite all the planning, the forces didn't exactly equal a professional army. And the overall expectations shifted from seizing Montreal to probing the enemy lines along the frontier.

From the outset, the Americans started off from a position of strength. The flanks of the army were secure. With elements of almost two full regiments of militia in Swanton, a thrust could have been ordered from Vermont into the Canadian towns east of Missisquoi Bay. While this was never seriously considered in the fall of 1812, it would be on the agenda in 1813 and again in 1814. The left flank was equally strong. In upstate New

York, the October 23 edition of the *Plattsburgh Republican* reported that New York militia had moved into position along the village of St. Regis. After a minor engagement, a small number of Canadian militiamen were captured, and the New York units held the border.[96]

Finally, and perhaps most importantly, the navy was ready. By Friday, October 25, the sloops *President* and *Hunter* were approaching Plattsburgh, preparing to support the troops as they moved north. The *President*, originally the *Fox*, was the largest, most well-armed vessel on the lake. At over sixty feet long and carrying an armament of six eighteen-pound cannons and two twelve-pounders, it alone could have blunted any British naval activity. It was more maneuverable than any of the smaller British ships and better armed. In temporary command of the *President* was Captain Billings. The Americans had erected defensive block houses along the northern edge of the lake, and bateaux patrolled between the Rouses Point and Alburgh. The sloop *Hunter* arrived on October 30, fresh from a refit at Whitehall. The *Hunter* effectively doubled the American naval advantage on Lake Champlain, armed with an eighteen-pound cannon and six six-pounders. Lieutenant Sydney Smith commanded the vessel.[97]

The foliage started to fall, trees revealed their naked branches and colder temperatures set in. During the first weeks of November, the regular army units stationed around Plattsburgh were ordered to the frontier. As late as November 5, the *Burlington Sentinal* reported 1,500 fighting men in Vermont, stationed between far off Derby, Burlington and Swanton.[98] Some elements of Clark's Eleventh Regiment, which had been stationed in Swanton since before the start of the war, also moved out with the militia.[99] The bulk of Bloomfield and Dearborn's army began northward.

Much of Fifield's and Williams's regiments were ordered to depart Swanton and move across the lake.[100] There are no known historical accounts that detail the troop movements as they left town, but their journey to support the invasion is easily tracible. Stationed in the center of the village for months, several hundred men suddenly needed large numbers of the bateaux. There were no bridges constructed across the Missisquoi River leading west. Nor were there bridges from Swanton to Alburgh in the Missisquoi Bay area.

The companies departed for upstate New York and took three or four possible routes, probably making use of all of them. Some departed the village after crossing at the ferry at what is today Ferry Street. This is just south of the area of the falls, and a ferry had been operated there since settlement began. The soldiers marched due west, along the rough-cut road recently constructed by Swanton resident Levi Scott. After a forty-five-minute march, they arrived at the open waters of Maquam Bay and boarded the bateaux and sloops awaiting them. From there, the fastest route to upstate New York would be a winding journey above North Hero, along the Alburgh Shore and then north of Isle La Motte. They connected with the main American invasion force massing at Champlain. It is also likely that some companies marched along Maquam Bay and assembled at what is known as Clark's Point, in West Swanton. The other two paths of departure involved the Missisquoi River and relied on bateaux. The soldiers boarded the bateaux and followed the river north into the open waters of Missisquoi Bay. Some landed in Alburgh, marched through town and assembled on the western shore at Windmill Point.[101] This location gave immediate and quick access to Rouses Point and Champlain on the New York side. Finally, with an entire invasion underway, in concert with the navy and the use of bateaux, it is likely small numbers of scout vessels were sent north into the bay. American bateaux would have sown confusion among British pickets and scouts in St. Armand, Phillipsburg and the area south of Isle Aux Noix. The northern stretches of the bay lay in Canada, only a few miles from the British fortification.

A few men were left in Swanton, and they continued to deal with smuggling. Two separate incidents were reported in the town of Huntsburgh, present-day Franklin, in early November.[102] It is not known which companies were moving back and forth between Swanton and Derby, still patrolling and monitoring the frontier.

In Plattsburgh, all of the military regiments departed their encampments and set out for Champlain, right on the border. These units included the Sixth, Ninth, Eleventh, Fifteenth, Sixteenth, Twenty-First and Twenty-Fifth regular infantry regiments, as well as artillery and cavalry units.[103] The Vermont and New York militia units crept toward the border in support. By the second week of November, most of the force was positioned just a half mile from enemy territory. Scouting parties were sent out and returned with information that trees had been felled along the main roads.

And then things began to fall apart.

First, poor intelligence forced Dearborn to vastly overestimate the size of the enemy directly in his path. Contrary to the earlier published accounts of the time, there were only three hundred native warriors allied to the British in the woods north of the Canadian border towns. Additionally, while the roads to Isle Aux Noix had been blocked with downed trees, the size of the British regular army force was in fact very limited. The Americans were opposed by just a few companies of De Salaberry's militia. There were

Northern Vermont in the War of 1812

Area of the Missisquoi Bay bridge between Swanton and Alburgh. *Photo by Armand Messier of northernvermontaerial.com.*

Windmill Point in Alburgh. The 1812 American invasion of Canada assembled in upstate New York. *Photo by Armand Messier of northernvermontaerial.com.*

Northern Vermont in the War of 1812

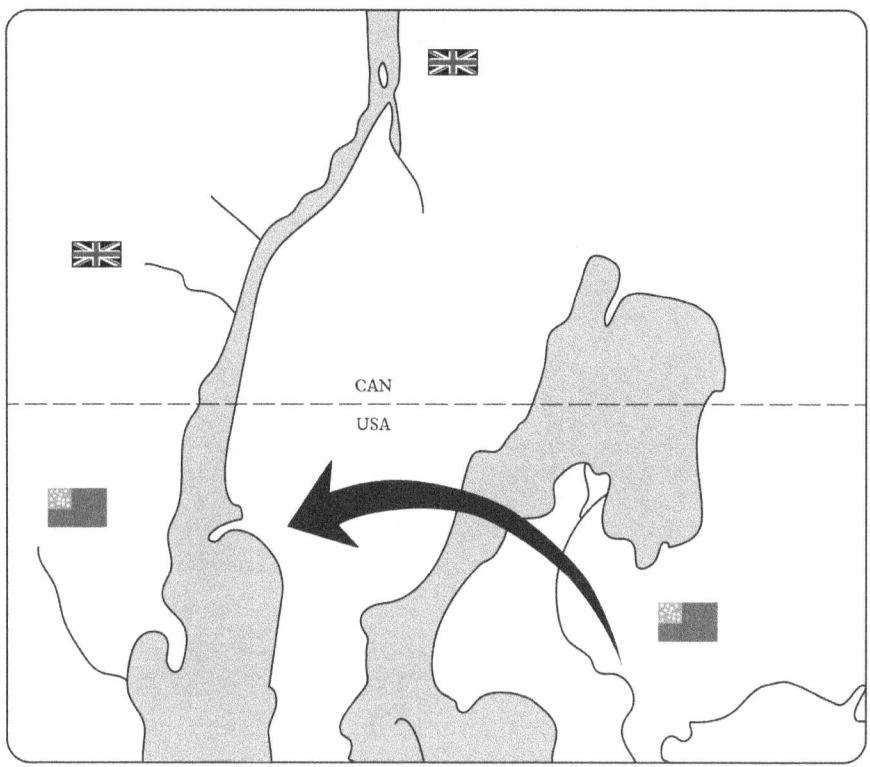

Vermont militia units were willing to cross the lake, but not the border. *Artwork by Lindsay DiDio.*

nearly five thousand American soldiers on the border by November 17. They were up against scattered bands of Indians and militia that might have totaled five hundred. The Americans believed there was a much larger force directly in front of them, and it caused delays all along the line.

Next, if weather, poor planning and disease hindered the invasion, the reality of what the militiamen were being asked to do finally hit home. They were camped in Champlain, New York, waiting for the offensive to commence. However, many of the Vermonters arriving at the line noted their service did not require them to leave U.S. territory.[104] The refusal to go into Canada was led by many of the men from Fifield's regiment and spilled over to Williams's regiment.[105] The *Plattsburgh Republican* reported that nearly half of Fifield's men refused to go any farther. Marching through the snow-covered fields of Quebec in November and December, after not being home to support their families at the end of the fall growing season, was an unacceptable choice. Their decision sowed insubordination in the ranks and spread distrust and resentment of the militia. Area newspapers reported that militia men also disobeyed orders due to the lack of winter clothing.[106]

The actions and bravery of the Canadian militia, who were fighting to defend their homes, is magnified when measured against the force they opposed. Fortunately for them, the American effort was half-hearted, bumbling and unorganized.

The last of the armed American sloops, the *Bulldog*, had arrived after being outfitted in Whitehall, and its armament further cemented American superiority. *Hunter* and *President* had already pushed northward and were hugging the shores of Rouses Point, just west of Alburgh. *Bulldog* carried an eighteen-pound cannon, two twelve-pounders and four six-pounders. Also sailing northward and joining the flotilla were the two converted gunboats, now effectively scows, each carrying a twelve-pound cannon.[107] The English gunboats were bottled up in the Richelieu.

Most of the American army crossed the border and approached the Lacolle River on the morning of November 20. As the hours passed and his men moved forward, Dearborn understood that his chances of reaching Montreal were diminishing by the hour. Some historians speculate that the general's confidence had already wavered, and the objective may have shifted to taking Isle Aux Noix.[108]

Colonel Clark's men were responsible for the initial scouting assessments and they brushed up against the Canadian Voltigeurs and De Salaberry's First Battalion of Select Embodied Militia. In reserve, miles away from the first of the American probing actions, there were detachments of the Canadian Fencibles Regiment.

On the night of November 19, Colonel Zebulon Pike and the Fifteenth Regiment moved forward. Clark's scouts had detected a contingent of the Kahnawake Mohawks, just over the Lacolle River, opposite a dismantled bridge, taken down to slow the American advance. Pike's men and elements of Clark's forces approached the makeshift huts and guardhouse on the Lacolle River.[109] It snowed at points that night, although it did clear as the soldiers approached the river. Another Canadian unit entered the mix as squads of Canadian Voyageurs arrived to defend the woods near the Kahnawake Mohawk position. As Pike's soldiers reached the river, volleys were exchanged, and the outnumbered Canadians and English withdrew. Having crossed the Lacolle at another location, some of Clark's men were also approaching the guardhouse and huts. There was a friendly fire incident between the American units, with multiple casualties, including two deaths.

Another attempt was made to ford the river a little farther east, but the Americans withdrew after torching a few buildings.

And that was it.

Dearborn called off the offensive, and his army began to return to the area just north of Plattsburgh on November 20. The grand strategy of the Americans of walking into Canada had failed massively, with the hapless third prong of the invasion perhaps the least damaging. With the defeat of two separate armies earlier, perhaps the Americans could count themselves lucky to have avoided a major defeat in the Champlain theater.

Things continued to get worse, not better.

Many of the Vermont militia companies disbanded and started home, their enlistments expiring in late November and early December. The lack of commitment from the Vermonters, particularly from those in Fifield's and Williams's regiments, was a stinging indictment of the war effort. Not only was the northern frontier a hot bed of smuggling activity with the enemy, but local militia soldiers also refused to support their own national army. The U.S. regulars now moving back to Plattsburgh and Burlington had to cope with the disloyalty of a large percentage of locals and the apathy of many more.

The diseases that had started to take hold in October began to ravage the Champlain Valley in November. One contributing reason for the ineffectiveness of the army was how much the sickness had spread while the invasion attempt was underway. Press reports indicate that as many as seven hundred soldiers may have already fallen ill by late November.[110] Plattsburgh and Burlington were already housing concerning numbers of those too ill to report for duty. While the situation was not a full-blown epidemic yet, conditions were not sanitary, and militiamen returning to Vermont had been exposed to sick soldiers during the campaign.

One example of the hardships facing the region is the background story of Stephen Pettis, one of the company commanders from Williams's regiment. He had been stationed in Swanton throughout the fall. On November 7, as Pettis and his fellow Vermonters moved across the Missisquoi River into Alburgh to support the invasion attempt, he missed the birth of his newborn son. His wife, Cindy, died on November 22 as the militia units were returning home.[111]

The departure of the militia from the front was not a mass panic. The exodus of soldiers quickened with their enlistments expiring. However, the continued threat of the diseases also hastened the militia's desire to get home. Many took the same routes they had used to arrive for service. The

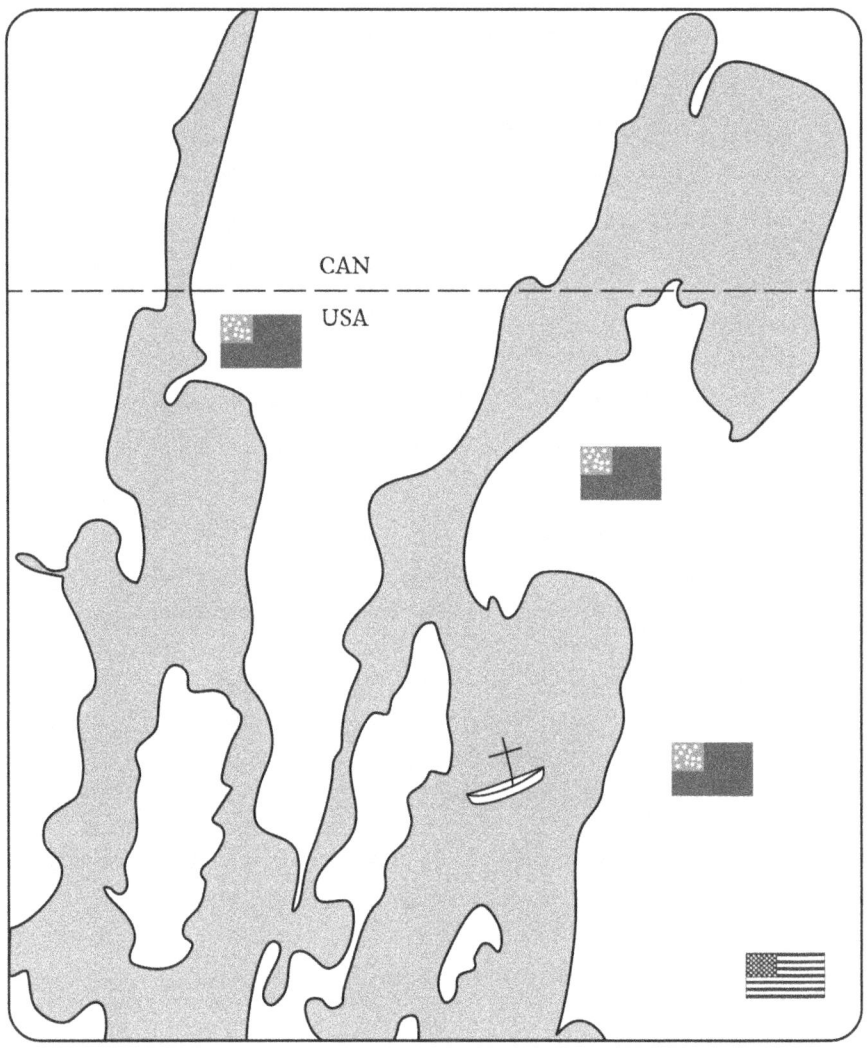

The Vermont militia units return home. *Artwork by Lindsay DiDio.*

bateaux and sloops were used again to get soldiers to the eastern shores of Lake Champlain. It is not known if the men of Phelps's company, Williams's regiment, who had originally been stationed in Swanton, were continuously used in their roles as seamen throughout November. Their enlistments ended around December 8.[112]

At least the militia units had homes to go home to. That was not yet the case with the regular army units stationed in Plattsburgh over the winter.

The forces set to return to Burlington were in a little better position. The cantonment in the area purchased by Colonel Clark was almost done by early December. Plattsburgh was a different story. Captain John Scott's letters from the fall again provide detail as to the plight of his men. He wrote in early December that there were few tents and that soldiers slept on the ground wrapped in blankets. The snow was already six inches deep, and the huts would not be ready for weeks.[113]

Edward Fifield's and William Williams's regiments returned to Swanton, likely through Alburgh and then over the ferries operating on Missisquoi Bay. Williams's regiment was discharged on or around December 8. Fifield's regiment, who had enlistments lasting throughout the winter, took over the duties at the cantonment in Swanton. His unit was also reorganized. The enlistments of Dodge's and Durkee's companies ended, and those men proceeded home. Most of Sam Wheeler's company stayed throughout the winter, and the remaining companies retained solid complements as temperatures fell and snowfall covered Franklin County. One addition to the regiment was Simeon Wright, who had served in Martindale's regiment during the excursion into Quebec.[114] It is unclear how many men Wright brought with him from the earlier command, but squads of his original company may have been merged with squads from Wheatley's original company. As these troops settled in for the cold winter, some newspapers published decidedly antiwar positions. The *Washingtonian* openly asked citizens to consider if the entire mission had been a waste of time, tax dollars and men.[115]

It was a different time of the year, but the duties were the same. Even though the possibility of an invasion in the winter was remote, men stationed in Swanton still needed to patrol the frontier. They also needed to tackle the smuggling situation and deal with the spreading diseases. On December 12, Fifield ordered Simeon Wright and a contingent of militia to guard the roads leading into Canada.[116] This made little difference, as they dealt with smugglers numerous times.[117] It also didn't stop his men from skirting over the border in large numbers to illegally enjoy establishments in Quebec. A Montreal newspaper wrote, "Fifty or sixty Americans, from Swanton Vermont, in a frolic, passed the lines to an inn, where they drank a bucket of gin sling, which they paid for, struck up the tune of Yankee Doodle, and retired peaceably. They were well equipped."[118] The regiment had to patrol the vast stretch of land between Lake Champlain and Lake Memphremagog. By the second week of December, Fifield's command had been reorganized into six companies. Half of this detachment was sent to the barracks in the Northeast Kingdom, ordered to keep an eye on the Canadian militia operating just over the border in the Stanstead Townships.[119] These men patrolled the roads from Memphremagog to the Troy area, just east of Richford. Fifield, headquartered at the Swanton barracks, had three companies to secure approximately thirty miles of border. It was an impossible task.

While not a retreat, the effort to get the men home wasn't without incident. The severity of the diseases continued to worsen and dominated the communities as much as cold temperatures for the next several months. Lifted of their need to support the failed invasion, the *President*, *Bulldog* and *Hunter* aided in the troop transportation home, along with the three other sloops and two scows. As seen in the months prior to the invasion attempt, safety was a concern as the bateaux were used to transport men home through bad weather and freezing temperatures. One accident happened at some point in December, when there was a collision on the lake between two or three bateaux. Several men drowned.[120] As the campaign season came to a close, MacDonough's fleet was ordered down to Shelburne Bay, just south of Burlington for winter quarters.

6
WAR IS COLD AND UNFORGIVING

WINTER 1812–1813

The weather continued to be difficult. Dr. Mann described the temperatures as "very cold."[121] The condition of the troops in Plattsburgh and Burlington continued to deteriorate due to combination of disease and cold. The civilian population of Vermont did not fare much better, as some militia members were already sick on their return journeys.[122] In most cases, the journey home took days. Each night that an ill soldier spent in someone's house or tavern increased the chances of spreading illnesses. A specific instance was reported in Vergennes, where discharged militia arrived in town but were too ill to travel home.[123]

During December, Dr. Mann took the opportunity to pen a letter to the press to clarify information that he believed had been incorrectly slanted by the *Washingtonian* newspaper. While it showed initiative by Mann to set the record straight, it highlights a very critical editorial slant by some newspapers of the time. The Burlington and Plattsburgh papers tended to publish accounts favorable to the U.S. military, regardless of the circumstances. The *Washingtonian* and others portrayed events in a negative light. Mr. Mann's letter was published by the Burlington paper on December 24, Christmas Eve. He stated that it was a version of the measles that first infected the camps in Plattsburgh, and conditions only got worse from there. Mann reported that the men were seized with "coughs" and "suffered many influences." The letter served as a public health alert.

Some of the regular army men supposed to quarter in Burlington for the winter were too weak to make the journey across the lake from Plattsburgh.

There was speculation that the frigid, unsanitary conditions in late November were a contributing factor to the spread of the ailments. For those soldiers who reached Burlington, the situation was deteriorating. On a single day in late December, 18 men were reported to have died. On a separate morning, 9 men were found dead in their tents.[124] In some cases, sick and diminished soldiers were settling into their new wooden huts even before the plaster was dry. By one account, 5 to 12 soldiers died each day. As the calendar switched to winter, the plight of Colonel Clark's Eleventh Regiment was particularly bad. The total fighting strength was supposed to be about 670 men. Of those, over 400 were too sick to report for duty.[125] The men were dying so quickly and at such concerning numbers that open pits were dug to throw the bodies in. In other cases, it was reported that full sleigh loads of sick soldiers and dead bodies arrived in Burlington.[126]

The units in Plattsburgh moved into Pike's Cantonment as soon as those buildings were finished, but that wasn't until Christmas. While they had waited, soldiers slept in tents in the snow, in many cases warmed by only a single blanket and cut branches of pine trees.[127] That men slept on frozen ground is an indictment of Generals Bloomfield and Dearborn, who had not initiated the process of erecting winter quarters earlier in the season. During the last portion of December, about one hundred of Pike's men succumbed to the diseases and died. Pike himself fell ill but recovered. Dr. William Beaumont did not attribute the worsening situation to any one cause but to "a great variety of diseases." Plattsburgh lost about 10 percent of the soldiers stationed there over the winter. Burlington lost a slightly higher rate of 12 percent. New York and Vermont communities also experienced great loss due to the illness, with one estimate putting the total number of deaths in Vermont at about five thousand.[128] Another estimate had the number well above six thousand.[129]

There is no concrete evidence that the diseases passing through the Champlain Valley affected Swanton and Franklin County worse than any other towns. Of all the soldiers in Fifield's Second Regiment, there were two recorded deaths while the men were stationed in Swanton.[130] The first was Samuel Bigsby of Vershire. He served in Oliver Taylor's Company. His enlistment started in September, but he passed away in December when the Second Regiment was returning to the Swanton Barracks. The second happened on December 22; the soldier was Ira Wilmington of Williamstown. He was listed as an indentured apprentice of Cornelius Lynde. Death visited the civilian population of the town as well, but not at a higher rate than other communities. Between December and early April, nearly two dozen people died in Swanton, but not all these deaths can be attributed to the outbreak ravaging the Champlain Valley.[131] Many deaths occurred in January and February, when the disease's influence was finally ebbing.

The situation was just as bad in southern Vermont. With members of the Vermont militia traveling back across the spine of the Green Mountains to get home, the south was not immune. Dr. Ware of Pomfret wrote, "In December last, the lung fever began, and continued to about the middle of May 1813. Thirty-four adults died with it in that time." He documented the bleeding and vomiting and noted that many people became ill but did not die. Other doctors noted the numbers in their towns. Arlington experienced ten known deaths. Sandgate had twice that number. Sixty or seventy died in Manchester. About forty people perished in Dorset, with a similar number in Rueport. Other towns like Pownal and Bennington recorded over seventy deaths each.[132]

The diseases and death were experienced not only by the Americans. Diseases ravaged the Canadian communities along the border throughout the season, with spotted fever being identified as the primary cause of death.[133]

As winter went on and the military leaders mulled over the events of the previous fall, pressure was applied to reduce the persistent cross border activity. On January 4, Captain Edward Toby of the U.S. Army stationed in Burlington prodded Fifield to push harder against illegal activity.[134] Fifield heeded the message and put more manpower behind the effort, as on January 8 he sent elements of Morrill's company to work the border in Richford.

There was no significant military action by either army in January, February or March 1813. The new year started out quietly for the Champlain Valley, as both the British and the Americans were likely licking their wounds from the extent of the disease that hit the area. General Prévost, the commanding general in Canada, didn't alter his defensive plans. He did not have the manpower to invade and could not hold significant portions of American territory. His strategy in the Great Lakes region was similar. The English in Canada needed to wait until larger forces could be sent from Europe. Until they arrived, the army would only seize the opportunity and go on the offensive in situations where English naval prowess could be brought to support military operations.

As the weather began to clear, the recovering military units at Burlington began to drill for a potential spring campaign. To the surprise of many, they were ordered out of the region.

7

THE CALM BEFORE THE STORM

Spring 1813

The Champlain Valley was emerging from winter, and the spread of the harsh diseases through the colder months had finally come to an end. As the snow melted and the planting season arrived in late April and early May, some of the frustrations of militia service were absent. In the fall, one of the biggest gripes with the invasion had been how it coincided with the harvest. Soldiers had been unable to bring in their crops. No such issues turned up on the Vermont side of the border in the spring of 1813.

In late March, the soldiers stationed in Burlington began another trek across the lake. This time the objective was not Montreal but western New York. As early as March 26, some of the detachments stationed in Plattsburgh were also underway. The Sixth Regiment was one of the first to leave. In a relatively short amount of time, the Ninth, Twenty-First and parts of the Twenty-Sixth had moved across the lake from Burlington.[135] American commanders stripped the Champlain Valley of much of its military presence. Significant forces were pushed west early in 1813 to Sacket's Harbor, New York, to expel the enemy from the region.[136]

That plan would change in a few short months.

As March changed to April, life was temporarily falling into a deceptive quietness in Northern Vermont that harkened back to the simple days of smuggling before the war.

Communities were nervous about the lack of military presence in the region. In Swanton, no major concentration of militia or regular army forces were stationed at the barracks since most of Fifield's Second

Regiment departed on March 17. With their enlistments complete, nearly the entire unit dispersed. The few who remained stayed because of physical limitations, still too ill to make the journey home. A select few were called upon to be the advanced guard for the northern frontier.[137] With the days getting longer, the focus of the average Vermonter was on the coming growing season, not on the war effort. So little was happening with the war effort that tensions began to rise between Vermonters and military units in the area. When there was a perceived enemy at the gates, it was perfectly acceptable to have the military around. However, for a time the war was far off and militia and regular army soldiers were reduced to border patrols. This was not a good recipe for a region that already resented the military presence to begin with.

On April 8, an account of John Hubbard of Huntsburgh was published in the *Washingtonian*. The paper reported that Hubbard, a U.S. citizen, was seized without a warrant in January, then imprisoned in the Swanton guardhouse. Before due process was applied, he was transferred to the Burlington base, where he was not given a trial. Issues were raised about the treatment of Hubbard, who was then marched back to Swanton and handed over to civilian authorities. While mysterious and unfortunate, the issue may not have received any attention except Hubbard was involved in Huntsburgh's local government and had even been town representative to the state legislature. When the situation hit the press, Fifield, whose men were responsible for the detainment, responded with his own letter to the paper. The colonel's response was to the point. He had ordered Ensign Gillman and a squad to Huntsburgh to patrol the roads leading to Canada. Hubbard, regardless of his status within the town, was involved with trade over the border and needed to be charged.[138] Nevertheless, the detention of a prominent citizen without due process intensified resentments and did little to cast military units in the region in a positive light.

Especially when it happened more than once.

In April, area resident Elisha Sears had been trading tobacco and other goods between the border towns and Burlington. When a Lieutenant Edson of the military stopped and questioned him, Sears did not want to be stopped and pushed the officer to the ground. At the time, there was no further incident. Later, Sears was briefly employed by a third party in Hunstburgh and received legal authority to travel into Canada in search of a horse thief. When he returned, Colonel Fifield arrested him. Sears did not immediately cooperate and was detained. He sat in the Swanton guardhouse for a week, then was sent to Burlington under military guard and imprisoned there for a few more weeks. Finally, Judge Paine, a local magistrate, released him without further incident.[139]

A few other happenings mark the mood within northwestern Vermont during the spring. Colonel Williams and his adjutant, who commanded the first of the units in Swanton the fall before, were court-martialed for their suspected role in smuggling activities.[140]

Another interesting sequence of events revolve around the sloop *Juno*. The sloop's association with the federal government goes back to when government assets were being moved into the region. It had been selected as one of the six vessels the army and navy purchased in the fall of 1812. Too small to warrant being armed, it made multiple trips between Burlington and Plattsburgh packed with men and supplies. However, its use during the fall was discontinued as the military campaign ended. After December, *Juno* fell into the hands of smugglers. In January and February 1813, *Juno* was discovered adrift off the coast of Plattsburgh, each time packed with goods linked to nefarious individuals. In May, the federal government was fed up with the situation and seized the vessel, forcing forfeiture on its owners.[141]

With the ice off Lake Champlain, MacDonough pushed his sloops north to patrol. With no U.S. military on the border in Vermont, he reported large amounts of cattle streaming into Quebec, probably information gathered from Swanton and the nearby border towns.[142] *President, Bulldog* (now the *Eagle*) and *Hunter* (now *Growler*) had been upgraded and received better armaments. MacDonough had all three vessels and the two scows in Plattsburgh by April 30. The cat-and-mouse games with the black marketers were underway again. The most important reason for the boats' move north had to do with Isle Aux Noix. The not-so-distant enemy installation was getting considerable attention from the English command, and it did not go unnoticed by the Americans. With the early portion of the fighting season approaching, the British were attempting to upgrade their facilities on the island. The naval yard was being expanded, and defensive positions on either side of the Richelieu were reinforced.

Responding to an appearance of British ships on the lake, the *Growler* and *Eagle* moved to a position between Plattsburgh, Alburgh and Rouses Point in late May.[143] The *President* was unavailable because she took significant damage after running aground earlier in the month. MacDonough's orders about not entering the Richelieu stood, and the two American sloops were not supposed to pursue. While it was believed *Growler* and *Eagle* would hold their own against the collection of vessels the British had, the narrows of the Richelieu River prevented the superior American craft from maneuvering well.

For the Americans, the worst-case scenario unfolded in the first days of June.

British gunboats appeared just north of the line on June 1, but initially the Americans did not bite. The *Growler* was commanded by the ever-eager Sidney Smith, the *Eagle* by a Mr. Loomis. With the appearance of the British gunboats, Smith believed he had the authority to engage and the firepower to win, so he signaled Loomis to pursue. Loomis initially resisted, due to a south wind, but eventually followed orders.[144]

The American pursuit went well, at first. The sloops crossed the border and had visual contact with three of the English gunboats near Ash Island.[145] These gunboats were probably the same three that were brought to Isle Aux Noix in the fall of 1812, the *Beresford*, the *Brock* and the *Popham*. In a battle on the lake, the American sloops would have run circles around the smaller, slower enemy ships. They had superior cannons, and it would have been a short fight. That advantage was neutralized when Lieutenant Smith ordered *Growler* and *Eagle* farther north. Still believing victory was within his grasp, Smith had been baited into shallower and narrower waters.

The Richelieu River is not deep near Isle Aux Noix, especially near the shores. The British realized their sudden good fortune, and while the American vessels tried to engage north of Ash Island, the British brought down wildly superior firepower. Isle Aux Noix was garrisoned by elements of the Royal Artillery, whose primary duty involved manning the cannons on the installation. Along with the engineers and workers on the island involved in upgrades, there were six companies of the 100th Regiment, commanded by George Taylor.[146] The three British gunboats were ordered to re-engage the sloops, now a much easier target.[147] As fire was exchanged between the two American ships and the three British vessels, the British brought up infantry on both banks of the Richelieu River. They poured musket fire at the crews of the *Growler* and *Eagle* while the gunboats advanced. The cannonade continued for nearly four hours, with the British ships slowly zeroing in on the desperate Americans. At around 11:00 a.m., a British shot critically damaged the *Eagle*, and it came to rest on the bottom in shallow water. The *Eagle* was boarded, and the crew surrendered. The *Growler* was unable to escape and called it quits about fifteen minutes later.

Nearly one hundred Americans were captured, but the stinging loss was the sloops. They had given the Americans superiority on Lake Champlain for the last ten months. Isle Aux Noix had been an isolated outpost with little chance of confronting a larger force to the south. Now the Americans had made a critical mistake and basically gifted the British two well-armed sloops.

To make matters worse, the British collected intelligence from their prisoners and quickly became aware of the dire American position in the region. They confirmed there were few soldiers stationed at Plattsburgh, the damage to the *President* and the status of the Burlington cantonment. The British set out immediately to repair the captured prizes and renamed them *Broke* and *Shannon*. They would significantly enhance the British naval capability to strike on Lake Champlain. Prévost and his command officers realized the opportunity as well. Lake Champlain and northern Vermont were about to get a lot more attention.

With the loss of the two sloops, MacDonough spent little time licking his wounds. He could not afford to hesitate long, as one of his two scows (the former gunboats) was anchored next to the *President*, both receiving repairs. His only remaining vessel, the other scow, was hardly enough to compete with the prizes the British had just received, augmenting their own gunboats. Inaction on his part would effectively give the British free reign of the lake. Displaying zeal he had shown the previous fall when working with the army to refit the three government sloops so quickly, MacDonough started to rebuild his fleet.

At some point during late spring, probably right after the loss of his two sloops, MacDonough went to the privately owned merchant fleet to bolster his forces. His first acquisition was the fifty-ton sloop *Rising Son*, which had been on the lake for a few years. Elijah Boynton had been its owner, and it had been built in Essex, New York, in 1810.[148] Once the transaction was complete, MacDonough immediately had his men working, making room for cannons and trying to improve its maneuverability. Even with the addition of *Rising Son* (renamed *Preble*), which required weeks to upgrade, the lack of ships left the Champlain Valley dangerously exposed. MacDonough expanded his fleet further with the *Montgomery*, the *Wasp* and the *Frances*.[149] The selection of these vessels probably lies with the ships the military was already familiar with. They had seized the *Juno* only months before and were familiar with the *Champlain* and the *Jupiter* from the previous fall's activity. The question was time. Did the Americans have enough of it to rebuild and replenish their fleet?

To add insult to injury, the ever-constant smuggling persisted. On June 1, reports surfaced of active smuggling from Derby into Canada. Later in June, there were similar reports from Highgate.

8
A STORM HITS THE NORTHERN HUB

SUMMER 1813

The American maneuvers did not help their immediate defense of the region. With the departure of the regular army from Plattsburgh, the area was virtually undefended except for the units in Burlington. The Niagara frontier would see significant action during the summer of 1813. In Burlington, the troop totals were significant enough for large supply requisitions to be made. Nathan Haswell of the customs office noted there were 10,000 barrels of pork and about 3,500 barrels of flour available for the soldiers.[150]

The British ability to do fine naval work was on display during the last days of June and throughout July. *Growler* and *Eagle* were renamed *Broke* and *Shannon* after being brought into the shipyard at Isle Aux Noix. Prévost and the British military command realized the opportunity they had. There were considerable questions about what resources could be devoted to any thrust into Lake Champlain, but the availability of two combat worthy sloops drastically changed the British plans. In a short time, Isle Aux Noix was transformed into a valuable forward operating base. The gunboats had only allowed a defense of the island and an occasional flirtation with crossing the border. *Broke* and *Shannon* gave them a navy that could be used for striking well into Vermont and New York.

The specifics give amazing detail about British naval capabilities. Immediately following the June 2 incident where *Broke* and *Shannon* fell into their hands, Taylor, the commander of the Isle Aux Noix garrison, brought in resources from Montreal and St. Jean to get them seaworthy again.[151] A flurry of administrative and command decisions followed, all centered on obtaining the necessary manpower to operate them. Plans were made to strike into American territory. The men who put the expedition together kept Prévost informed. In overall command of the preparations was Thomas Everard, from HMS *Wasp*, stationed along the St. Lawrence.[152] Any chance to drive a knife into the Americans through Lake Champlain would make the long-term goal of defending Montreal and Quebec easier. Daniel Pring was sent to Isle Aux Noix to manage the naval preparations. Lieutenant Colonel John Murray of the 100th Regiment of Foot, the commander of the forces at St. Jean, was given command of the soldiers involved in the coming offensive. His orders were to destroy military property on either side of the lake and to capture any vessels during the venture. This was a strategy in response to MacDonough's recent activity, where he had constantly turned private craft into military vessels with frustrating ease.

The force they assembled was a collection of the assets available and reflected just how thin the Montreal area defenses were. In late July, Prévost ordered Pring and Murray to proceed with an attack. About 1,000 men boarded forty-seven bateaux and were supported by the sloops *Broke* and *Shannon* and three gunboats.[153] Captain Everard helped plan the raid. The men came from a variety of different units: 24 came from the Royal Regiment of Artillery under the direction of Captain Gordon and were used to man the cannon on ships. The strike force consisted of 189 men from the 13th Regiment of Foot commanded by Colonel Williams, 234 of the 100th Regiment of Foot commanded by Taylor and 271 from the 103rd of Foot under the command of Smith;[154] 35 Canadian Fencibles and 35 Select Embodied Militia were also involved.[155] The men from the 100th of Foot were from Colonel Murray's unit and had been stationed at St. Jean and Isle Aux Noix since the war began. The Canadian Fencibles and Embodied Militia participated because of their knowledge of the towns along the frontier. The 103rd had a reputation of bad conduct and is said to have been made up of hardened criminals.[156]

They entered American waters on July 29, and the first act was to stop at the American customshouse at Windmill Point in Alburgh. Dr. James Wood, the agent there, sent word to General Wade Hampton, stationed in Burlington, that the British were on the move. Several of the British bateaux descended upon Wood in his small boat and took him prisoner.[157] He remained captive during the entire expedition and was imprisoned afterward. The British then moved south and began their first real offensive on Lake Champlain up to that point in the war.

Windmill Point in Alburgh. Militia units and military vessels were constantly in this area. *Photo by Armand Messier of northernvermontaerial.com.*

The strike was impressive based on what the British and Canadians accomplished. On July 30, the flotilla was off the coast of Chazy, and a contingent of soldiers went ashore. Murray issued a proclamation stating that individual citizens and private property would not be harmed if people stayed in their homes. They were off Plattsburgh on Saturday, July 31. It was not an invasion force. It was a raid designed to take advantage of almost no U.S. military forces stationed in upstate New York or Vermont. The new moon had been on July 27, a sliver of a crescent was visible on the western horizon.[158]

The bateaux rowed into Plattsburgh Bay and landed along the Saranac River. The larger ships took position to the south, keeping an eye toward Burlington where MacDonough's fleet was under repair. Enduring the scorching hot late July weather, the English and Canadians destroyed the arsenal, storehouses and blockhouse in Plattsburgh. Pike's cantonment was burned. A dangerous level of activity unfolded at Plattsburgh when some homes were looted and private property was carried away or stolen. The English soldiers spent an uncomfortable night deployed in enemy territory. The New York militia in the region was called out.[159] By the time Murray's soldiers departed, about three hundred militia had mustered three miles outside of town.[160] In Plattsburgh Bay, the merchant sloop *Burlington Packet* was seized; the thirteen-ton ship had been doing business between Burlington and Plattsburgh. It is not known if it had been in the service of the U.S. government during this time, but this was the first act in a plan that had two purposes. First, the British wanted to deny MacDonough the private vessels he had continuously made use of to augment the size of his fleet. By taking control of some of them, the British were effectively blunting the American navy's ability to rebuild itself. Second, if the overall raid was a success, they could turn the tables and do the very same thing. The *Burlington Packet* was filled with loot from the raid on Plattsburgh. On the morning of August 1, a storehouse on Cumberland Head was destroyed and the store of Matthew Saxe was burned at Chazy Landing. As with the spies who operated on the eastern shore of the lake, Plattsburgh had its own citizens who funneled information to the British. One of them, Joel Ackley, was exposed when a sweating Colonel Murray removed his hat in the August heat. In so doing, he accidently dropped a sheet of paper from the informant. Ackley had suggested ways for the British to hit Plattsburgh and provided information on the American boats in Burlington. After the British had departed, the paper was found and Ackley was confronted and arrested.[161]

The British departed Plattsburgh in their bateaux on August 1, aware that a detachment of local New York militia had been raised to confront them. At this point, the British force separated and the two smaller groups embarked on separate missions. This speaks to the confidence in their intelligence, as they would not have split their force if any serious American naval presence was on the lake.

As the hours of August 1 passed, the invading soldiers and their bateaux did not travel far. They crossed the narrow point of the lake south of Alburgh, with two of the three gunboats in support. The bateaux and gunboats landed at Sandy Point, near St. Anne's Shrine, on the island of Isle La Motte to spend the evening. They arrived prior to dark.

Isle La Motte residents Orlin Blanchard and John Parker attempted to observe the English force from the thickets along the shore. Blanchard had been stationed at the Swanton barracks between July 22 and December 9, 1812, along with twenty or so other men from Isle La Motte. They were discovered and spent the night as captives.[162] They learned one of the commanders of the British units was named Brisbane and that the raiders did not have significant knowledge of the islands or Vermont's eastern shore. There is no evidence the British actions on Isle La Motte resembled anything close to what happened in Plattsburgh. Scouts were posted, and information was gathered from the locals, but their target was a few miles away, along the shallow waters of Maquam Bay. The sun set after 8:00 p.m. The invaders had another half hour of graying dusk and then spent their second night in enemy territory. Parker and Blanchard were held all night. Dr. Wood of the Alburgh customs station endured his second night of captivity. The morning light on August 2 emerged just before 5:00 a.m. The black of night had lifted, but the British were about to descend on Swanton and bring dark clouds with them. Parker, Blanchard and Wood were forced to serve as guides. Isle La Motte resident Caleb Hill communicated with the captives while hiding in brush along the enemy encampment. The troops loaded on the forty-seven bateaux near dawn. They navigated the northern end of Isle La Motte and the southern edge of Alburgh. The British force proceeded east through the thin, shallow channel separating Alburgh from North Hero. The route through the islands took them on an extended north/southeastwardly journey in the shape of an *S*.

Meanwhile, *Broke*, *Shannon* and the final gunboat departed southward to see what damage they could inflict near Burlington. Captains Everard and Pring brought their sloops into the broad lake and approached

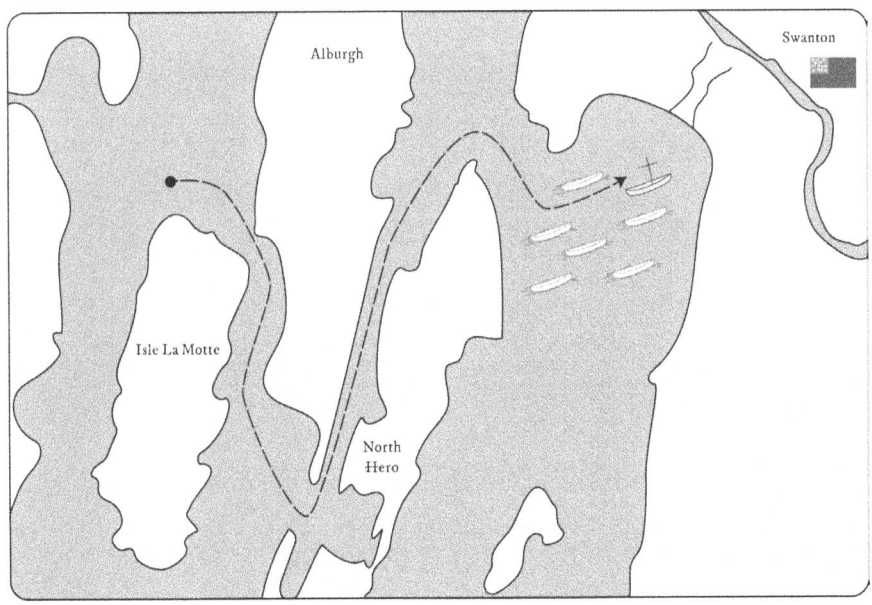

Path that the British took from Isle La Motte on their way into Swanton during Murray's Raid. *Artwork by Lindsay DiDio.*

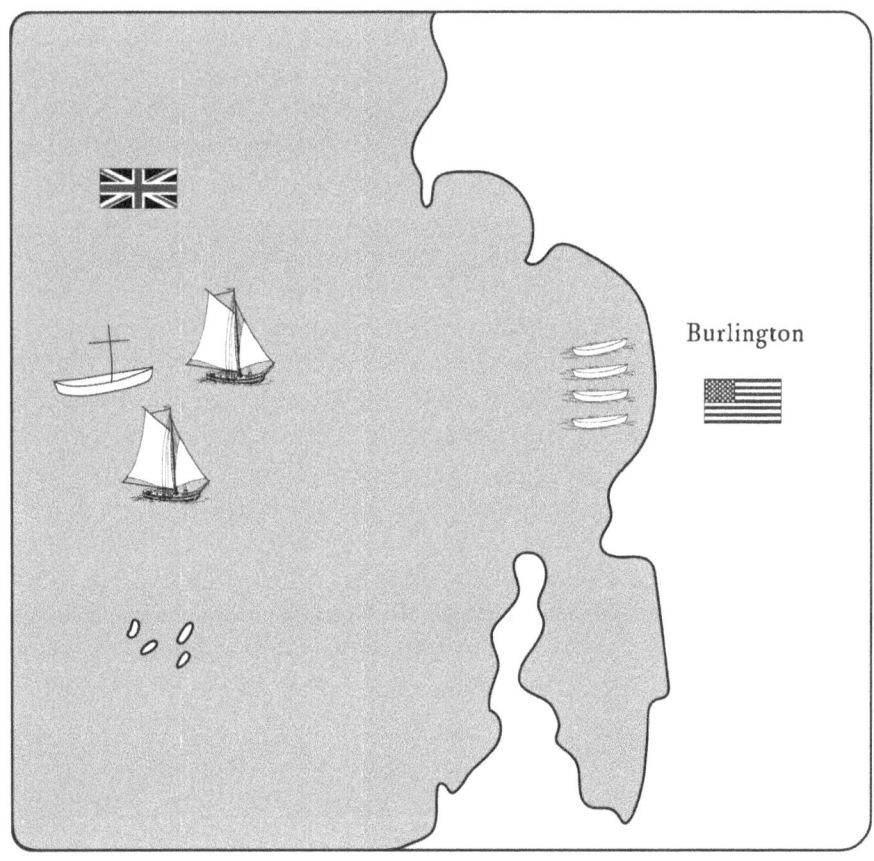

Murray's Raid in August 1813. British sloops threaten Burlington. *Artwork by Lindsay DiDio.*

Burlington by about 2:30 in the afternoon. The gunboat was slower and sailed behind the two larger vessels. As the ships approached Burlington, church bells sounding the alarm could be heard on the decks of the British ships. Seeing MacDonough's fleet in the Burlington docks, Pring identified three of the vessels being upgraded. Everard observed additional vessels under protection of the big shore guns.[163] Pring also noted American shipmen attempting to bring their heavy guns to bear. For the first time, the British were also able to observe the cantonment in Burlington, located on the high ground above the docks. American cannons began to fire from defensive positions along the shore.[164] The British returned fire, and a brief, long-distance battle ensued. The British hoped to goad MacDonough into the open water, away from the

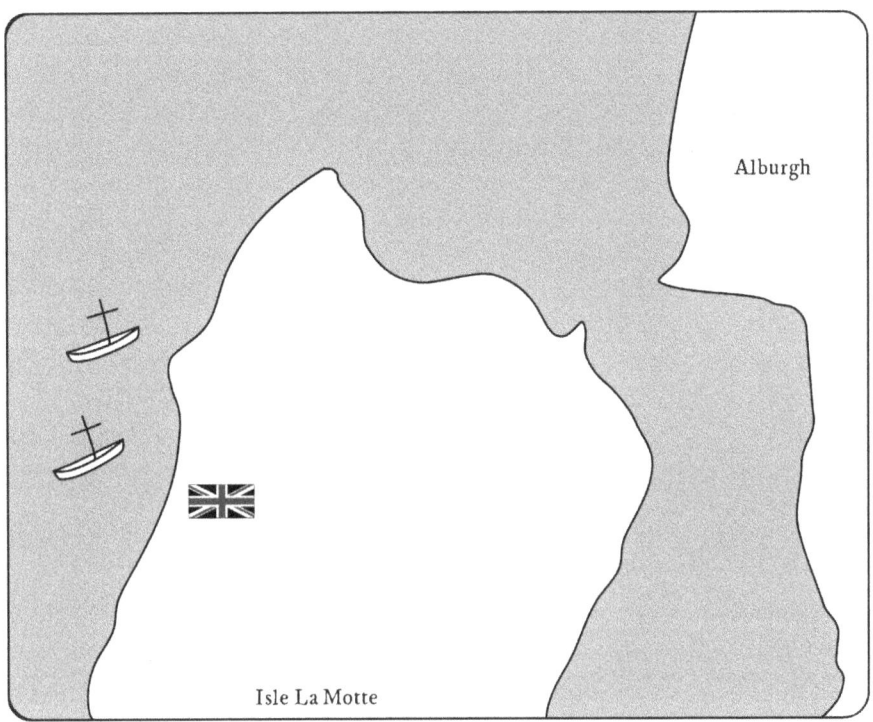

Part of Isle La Motte was occupied by the British for one night during Murray's Raid. *Artwork by Lindsay DiDio.*

cover of the supporting ground artillery. MacDonough did not take the bait, and his boats remained in Burlington Harbor. The fire between the two sides was basically ineffective. The American shots were in line, but the British successfully remained just out of range. The British fire was just as ineffective, with only one shot damaging a private home in Burlington. The situation in the nearby towns was understandably chaotic. Residents in the city retreated to Essex, Shelburne and other neighboring communities fearing a British landing. Rumors spread that the British had landed about two thousand troops in Colchester, just north of Burlington, and a few companies of American regulars were marched out to Mallets Bay to investigate.[165]

While the Americans were content to maintain their defensive position, the British set out to press their advantage. *Broke* and *Shannon* sailed a few miles farther south, looking to disrupt American shipping. The gunboat, still to the north, tagged along. The afternoon hours of August 2 were the most effective portion of the raid. While no American military vessels were affected, MacDonough's ability to call on merchant ships to replenish combat losses was severely diminished. Up to this point the only casualty had been the *Burlington Packet* up in Plattsburgh. The scope of the raid was about to get exponentially greater.

Over the span of the next few hours the British seized the ten-ton *Red Bird*, a Durham boat carrying flour for the government, the *Willing Maid* and *Federal Victory* at twenty tons, the *Lark* at fifteen tons and the much bigger *Essex*, *Enterprise* and *Mars*.[166] The sixty-ton *Essex* was one of the larger ships on the lake, and when the British had trouble piloting it, they burned the hull out in the open water.[167] The *Lark* had been used by the federal government during the smuggling days. The *Enterprise* was forty-five tons, the *Mars* thirty-five. Both prizes the British hoped to get back to Isle Aux Noix. When MacDonough offered no serious pursuit, the prospect of getting them back to Canada increased exponentially.

Meanwhile, at the northern end of the lake, the gunboats and the scores of bateaux were entering Maquam Bay, just west of Swanton. Accounts of the raid into the town are limited, most of them written years after the event. However, the layout of the lake and western shore of Vermont, along with the path of the Missisquoi River, give clues as to the flow of events on the morning of August 2.

At this point, the British were confident that the final portion of the raid was going to be a success. The force observed the area of Clark's Point in West Swanton, at the southernmost tip of the Missisquoi Delta. The area had been used by Isaac Clark and the American military detachments throughout the war. Based on the size of the English force and the available intelligence, the English kept an eye to the north, just in case there were unknown bateaux or militia inside Missisquoi Bay. There is no indication the British entered the isolated waters of Missisquoi Bay during the raid.

By mid-morning, the detachment had moved into Maquam Bay, near the southwest portion of Swanton. The two gunboats and the men from the Royal Regiment of Artillery took up a position away from land, covering the other ships with their cannon. Most of the bateaux went ashore, unloading their soldiers. Blanchard and Parker, the two Isle La Motte captives, remained on the boats. Colonel Murray noted in his letter later describing the expedition that his forces burned and destroyed several American bateaux "at the landing place."[168] Murray personally commanded the mission into Swanton, accompanying his soldiers into town. Several companies were left to guard the boats and secure the shore.[169]

View of Lake Champlain looking south from Franklin County. *Photo by Armand Messier of northernvermontaerial.com.*

Soaked by disembarking from the boats in two or three feet of water, the force went ashore and first encountered the Manzer property.[170] They forced "old man Manzer" to act as a guide and to disclose the quickest route to the barracks. One of the British officers, probably Murray or Williams, stole one of Manzer's horses and rode it while his column got underway. Manzer told them of two roads. The more suitable was longer, running along the Missisquoi River extending north–south toward St. Albans. It was a decently traveled wagon road, but the raiders had to go nearly a half a mile inland just to get to it. This road is likely Middle Road today. The second option was the road worked on by Swanton resident Levi Scott only months before. This path allowed a direct route into town from the bay but was not yet finished. It had been laid through land that was terribly marshy in sections, the stumps and roots not fully removed. This is present-day Lake Road.

The English opted to take the shorter path, experiencing ground nearly impossible to maintain formation over. A detachment of men was left at the shore to guard the boats. The several hundred soldiers soon found themselves stumbling over logs, tripping over roots and sinking knee-deep into the muddy, boggy ground. The effort was frustrating enough that Murray brought his pistol upon Manzer and threatened him, fearing his men were

Northern Vermont in the War of 1812

View of Lake Champlain looking south from Maquam Bay, just west of Swanton. *Photo by Armand Messier of northernvermontaerial.com.*

View of Maquam Bay from West Swanton. During Murray's Raid, forty-seven British bateaux and two gunboats anchored in the bay. *Photo by Armand Messier of northernvermontaerial.com.*

Northern Vermont in the War of 1812

Maquam Bay in Swanton. British soldiers would have departed from here for their raid into Swanton. *Photo by Armand Messier of northernvermontaerial.com.*

being led into a trap.[171] While British intelligence was good enough to strike into town, they could not have known patrol routes of the militia or the identities of patriotic citizens willing to take a shot at them. Not only was the road marshy, but thick woods also obscured lines of sight.

Filthy, sweating and with uniforms caked with muck and grime, they moved closer to town. They approached the winding Missisquoi River an hour or so after coming ashore. There was no bridge over the river in this region, but there was a ferry operating a few hundred feet above the dam, run by Swanton citizen Joel Carley. Murray aimed his pistol just above the ferry and fired into the sky to compel Carley to bring the scow to the western side. The ferry was maneuvered to the west bank, about thirty rods above the dam. The British believed this would be easier than storming across below the dam, where the water flows rapidly over rocky, dangerous ground. With the ferry under the soldiers' control, one large load of the raiding party moved across the Missisquoi River. It was this group that moved against the barracks, their number large enough to intimidate the townspeople, but only a portion of the total force that traversed the swampy road. Murray's decision to divide his forces is understandable. Exposed, in an enemy town with a military base in it, he decided to use speed over force. Use of the ferry meant multiple trips. If there were enemy units nearby, the British exit needed to be swift, so men were left near the Missisquoi to guard for a hasty retreat.

Members of the 103rd of Foot, under the command of Colonel Williams, were part of the group that torched the barracks.[172] These soldiers went after property and buildings suspected of being used by the American military. They took barrels of whiskey, pork, boxes of soap, candles and half a barrel of tallow. Two soldiers entered a tanner's shop near the rear of the village and removed the military equipment, clothing and calfskins.

The events that transpired when the British entered the main part of the village can be imagined based on the layout of the settlement. Those going after the barracks spread out on the east side of the river. The second group, which lay on the west side of the Missisquoi, waited to see billowing smoke on the horizon. When the smoke started to ascend, their mission would soon be over.

British soldiers rushed up the slight rise just beyond the banks of the Missisquoi, into the main section of the village, following Ferry Street up to the green. Many businesses and homes lay along the river, and soldiers kept an eye on emerging concerned citizens. No locals moved to prevent the raid. Intelligence gathered before the mission had revealed the barracks were empty, but the Englishmen spread out, pistols and muskets

View from Swanton overlooking present-day Lake Road. During Murray's Raid, the British ships were anchored in the bay. British soldiers approached the village from this location. *Photo by Armand Messier of northernvermontaerial.com.*

View of the Missisquoi River in the approximate location where the British soldiers crossed during Murray's Raid. *Photo by Armand Messier of northernvermontaerial.com.*

drawn, watchful of anyone willing to interfere. They then fanned out to the southeast section of town, wove through the small number of homes and approached the three barracks structures. The parade ground was bare of grass or brush. They ignited fires in several locations to speed the progress of the blaze. While this was underway, other men destroyed military-related property. The customshouse was likely a target, but there is no record it was torched.

It is unknown to what extent, if any, the redcoats harassed the family or property of Jabez Penniman, who had spent a good portion of his career working to prohibit trade along the border. British soldiers went to the "Old Brick Store" on the northeast shoulder of the village and moved to torch it when they discovered government provisions inside. Swanton resident Augustus Burt approached and informed the raiders that the federal government had forced the town to house the provisions. Since they had been ordered to respect private property, the English left the "Old Brick Store" alone but brought the government supplies outside and destroyed them not far from the burning barracks. The recruitment center set up by Isaac Clark and Valentine Goodrich was sacked, and they may have burned a hospital that was a part of the barracks.[173] Soldiers remained in the vicinity as the flames spread, fully engulfing the structures. Squads were posted along the roads to prevent anyone from entering the area. Some soldiers attempted to get sympathetic citizens to participate in the destruction of government property.[174]

Murray had been ordered to respect private property, especially in Vermont, considering how many citizens had been openly defying the U.S. government.[175] However, the looting that occurred at Plattsburgh started again, particularly by soldiers in units left on the lake side of the river. The actions of the British incursion closer to the lake, where companies anxiously waited, went less by the book. There is no evidence the British set about to damage this section of town, its businesses or the townspeople in any organized way. They did not take prisoners. Members of the community who had served in the militia in the fall of 1812 were probably closely watched. The British did not torch the bridge in the extreme southeast corner of town, which had been erected and used by the federal government. That road was a direct route to St. Albans and from there onto Burlington.

What happened with the waiting soldiers can also be imagined. The contingent that remained with the bateaux would have been on alert and nervously watched the horizon and tree line. The group that remained on the west bank of the Missisquoi River found differing ways to pass the time. Some scouted the roads, to watch for anyone advancing from the south. Others were ordered north, along the river, to search for other bateaux or government provisions.

The wait was undoubtedly nerve-wracking. Some of the men engaged in questionable activities. It is possible a portion of the 103rd of Foot remained in this area, its members violating homes and looting. Small indiscretions included the trampling of the Goodrich family garden and stealing some of their vegetables. In another instance, as the soldiers prepared to return to the boats, one footman stole a watch from a young Mr. Sowles. After the raid, depositions were filled out claiming that the British had indeed forced their way into homes, stealing household items like glasses, spoons, bowls and clothing. Farmers reported the British stole hens.[176]

Other accounts indicate Colonels Murray and Williams attempted to maintain as much control as possible over their men. There was an accusation against one soldier who looted the home of Levi Scott, brought by Swanton citizens Wanton Northrup and one other. When they brought their charges to the British colonels, the offending soldier received lashes in front of onlooking Swanton citizens. This was in line with military discipline of the time. However, more serious offenses were recorded.

Candis Asselstyne testified later that soldiers forcibly entered her home and looted almost everything her family had. Other troops remained outside and did nothing to interfere with the wrongs being committed. She provided a list of the stolen items in a sworn affidavit to Justice of the Peace Eleazer Brooks. The violations at the Asselstyne home also involved more than a dozen soldiers grabbing a fourteen- or fifteen-year-old dark-skinned woman working on the property. The men brought her into a room, and Mrs. Asselstyne reported hearing screams as the young woman was raped. In another household, there was a second attempted rape involving Mrs. Manzer, but she was reportedly able to fight her attackers off.[177]

With the barracks consumed by flames and most of the government provisions destroyed, the British force in the village returned to the ferry. They recrossed the river and assembled with the larger force. They avoided the muddy, tiring experience traveled earlier and used the wagon road spoken of by Mr. Manzer. The departure involved heading back up the small embankment just west of the Missisquoi and marching due south for about a mile. At that point, the wagon road intersected with another smaller road that took them directly back to the lake. It is said that the British attack lasted no more than three hours.

Loading into the bateaux and departing from Maquam, the British witnessed the fruits of their handiwork—the smoke reaching above the horizon. They rejoined the gunboats farther off shore and proceeded west, looking for the fleet returning from Burlington. They piloted the same narrow channels through the islands and deposited Blanchard and Parker back along the Isle La Motte shoreline. During the excursion on Lake Champlain and onto American soil, sixteen British soldiers deserted from the 103rd of Foot.[178] It is unclear if any of them took the opportunity to abandon their comrades while the raid in Swanton was underway.

The press accounts of the raid and the sworn depositions by citizens highlight the deep divisions that gripped Vermont. Some were written to spread the word of every offense committed, a reasonable and honest journalistic endeavor considering a war was on. Other newspapers, and some Swanton citizens, felt a duty to dispute the reported ills in the aftermath of the raid. In some cases, they accused those making the depositions of not understanding what they had reported, suggesting the claimants could not read or write.[179] For example, the *Washingtonian* disputed Mrs. Asselstyne's account of the reported rape on her property, saying the young woman was seized at one point—and that she did cry out in surprise—but that the British soldiers quickly released her. The implication was that those who took the deposition lead Mrs. Asselstyne into describing the worst things possible, to sway opinion against the British. Ohers challenged Mr. Northrup, who claimed to have witnessed the lashes given to a looting soldier. Another Swanton resident wrote the lashing was administered because the soldier attempted to flee the ranks of his unit.[180] Yet another account accused the British of threatening Swanton citizens with the points of their bayonets. When safely back in Quebec, Colonel Williams published his own account of the raid and disputed some of the harshest criticism. He confirmed that at least one soldier from the 100th Regiment had been flogged as the soldiers departed town. All in all, the British returned to Quebec knowing the attacks had been a big success.

Only months before, Swanton had been a staging area in support of the failed 1812 Quebec invasion. The British had every right to worry that the town could have been used again. With the completion of Murray's Raid, a thorn in their side close to the border had been removed. The American detachment in Burlington was fifty miles away and not an immediate threat.

The war would revisit the northern border for the next several months. While the British attack was a dazzling success, the American command came to understand that the Swanton area could be used as a point to bring constant pressure against the enemy.

The next phase of Swanton's involvement happened shortly after Murray's Raid. The American generals' attention had been on the Great Lakes much of the summer. What forces they did have in the Champlain Valley had been huddled in Burlington, available but not close to the enemy. As the calendar transitioned from August to September, U.S. troops were busy crossing Lake Champlain again. A brief incursion was made into southern Quebec, just north of Champlain, New York, but then nearly the entire American army remaining in the area was marched forty miles west, to Chateaugay.

In September and October 1813, the northwest corner of Vermont was once again brought into the back-and-forth action of the war. A good-sized American offensive into Canada was underway by September, when Generals Hampton and Wilkinson stumbled north from New York with an army of four thousand men.

The Swanton area became extremely nervous. There were few federal troops in the area, and the war had dragged on for over a year. In concert with the federal government, the Third Brigade of the Vermont militia, under the command of Luther Dixon, was mustered and moved over to Plattsburgh and Champlain, New York.[181] This did little to ease the nervousness of the Vermont frontier towns.

Another call-up of the Vermont militia, most of whom were from Franklin County, did not go well. For these men, it was the second deployment in less than twelve months. Of the nine hundred men called upon, a high number served little more than a week. Most only served one month and twenty-three days. Many had been lukewarm the first time they had been called upon, and now the harvest season approached once again. Of all who were mustered, only about three hundred stayed for the duration of their service.[182] This number represented barely one third of the total servicemen needed.[183] The men from Swanton who served were Shadrack Hathaway, Ezekiel Goodrich, Amasa Brown, Stephen Brown, Ira Church, Rufus Barney, Samuel Emery, Abraham Manzer and John Pratt. Eleven companies were called upon, but so few served that the remaining force was reorganized. They were first deployed to Burlington. After about a month, they were stationed in Plattsburgh at Cumberland Head.

MacDonough cobbled together all of the vessels under repair in Burlington and moved them to Plattsburgh by early September. The naval situation was drastically different than it had been only a few short weeks ago. With the *President, Montgomery, Preble, Wasp, Frances* and the two scows, his ships were at least a match for what was at Isle Aux Noix. The American fleet was again on the lines and hopefully preventing a repeat of Murray's Raid. The arrival of MacDonough's ships in the north also allowed the government to move against illegal behavior. Just after the scows reached the northern end of the lake, smugglers attempted to pass the flotilla and were stopped.[184]

On September 9, the two English sloops and three gunboats crossed the border in the area of Alburgh and Isle La Motte. They harassed shipping, seized one small boat and threatened the American military presence in upstate New York.[185] When MacDonough brought his fleet north, the British squeezed back into the Richelieu. On September 20, the five American sloops were just off Chazy, New York, supporting General Hampton's march to that village. The American vessels went back and forth between Plattsburgh and the border, hoping to provoke the British, as the British had done to the American vessels in June.

While most of the British troops involved in the Murray's raid excursion had been deployed elsewhere, there was a serious investment in the British presence on Lake Champlain underway, and it was happening fast. They renamed a few of the larger sloops captured in early August, and a vast shipbuilding campaign was underway. The merchant sloop *Mars* was converted to a fighting vessel and renamed *Canada*. Another received upgrades and was now the *Icicle*. The vessels were not yet ready, but in a short amount of time they might be able to match anything the enemy was able to deploy. The British started construction on another two gunboats, in addition to the ones already underway.[186] The American intelligence agent at Champlain reported this information.

The lack of commitment by the Vermont militia was comparable to the insubordination during the failed invasion attempt near Lacolle Mills the year before. American leadership remembered the previous campaign season when a large percentage refused to cross the border and might do so again. The unit reorganization occurred because of the quickly depleting ranks of the men. The military wanted support for the army moving north forty miles away in Chateaugay, New York. Flares of patriotism were shown among those who answered the muster call. Vermont governor Martin Chittenden did not fully support the use of the Green Mountain Boys outside of the state. He detested the prospect of Vermonters supporting an invasion into Canada and recalled the militia in late summer. But several companies, including many of the men from Swanton, refused to obey the governor's order. They remained in Plattsburgh and waited to see what the U.S. Army was planning.

Lack of faith in the army and navy was not just displayed by members of the Vermont militia. On or around September 29, the sloop *Wasp* docked at Plattsburgh. One of the crew, James Treadwell, described as a dark-skinned man with no prominent features, was reported absent without leave. A reward of ten dollars for Mr. Treadwell's capture and return was advertised in the local newspapers.[187]

In late September, Hampton, one of the new American generals, ordered Isaac Clark to create a diversion along Lake Champlain to support the overall campaign. He wanted a "petty war along Lake Champlain."[188] Clark was the obvious choice. He had set up the recruitment center in Swanton the summer before and dealt with the militia units throughout the fall and winter. Clark spent the late September days organizing his command. As he developed his plans, he requested his force be augmented by two companies of New York militia and sixty St. Regis Indians.[189] Apparently, this request was not honored. It is not known to what degree Clark relied on men of the Eleventh Regiment to fill out his ranks. Pressure was building for a diversionary attack on

Lake Champlain to commence, as command officer Elias Tatset received orders from General Parker to coordinate with Clark and move against the settlements north of Missisquoi Bay.[190] In a much different way than the previous year, northwestern Vermont was about to become a hub of activity again. Clark likely used some of the remaining elements of Luther Dixon's Vermont militia to support his plans for raiding into southern Quebec.

9
A PETTY WAR ALONG LAKE CHAMPLAIN

Fall 1813

A painful back and forth developed along the border. Small raiding parties from both sides struck numerous times. Isle Aux Noix was the headquarters for the British in the sparring, which lasted months. Plattsburgh and Burlington were the primary anchors of the American presence, but Swanton and the neighboring towns became a critical smaller hub.

Even with the American offensive underway near Chateaugay, the British gunboats returned to the border on October 7. They thrust out of the Richelieu and took any small craft they could find within three miles. The residents of Alburgh and the Lake Champlain islands were in constant fear of being occupied. This incident was in response to American aggression in upstate New York, where militia had attacked a small British force on the line.[191]

Isaac Clark's plans for his incursions were multilayered. The overall objective was to get to Montreal, but his focus was disrupting the Canadian towns along the border. Wilkinson and Hampton were trying to push north in New York but having little success. As the back and forth between the armies continued, if any of Clark's activities were wildly successful, American leadership might consider a move against Isle Aux Noix on their way to Montreal. As had become standard procedure with the American military on the border, Clark needed to cut down the constant smuggling as well.

On the night of October 11, Clark assembled a force of about four hundred men. He had cobbled together a joint navy and army force of one sloop, the two scows—each carrying a six-pound cannon—and ten bateaux. The sloop involved in the effort was likely the *Wasp*, *Frances* or *Montgomery*. It is doubtful the *President* or the *Preble*, the two largest American sloops, would have been assigned to the isolated waters of Missisquoi Bay. The force left just after sunset, sometime around six o'clock. They used the brightness of the waning moon to guide them away from the New York shore. The small flotilla traveled through the narrows between Isle La Motte, Alburgh and North Hero. The darkness concealed the effort, and the Americans took the same route through the islands that Murray's raiders had taken just two months earlier. In the early hours of October 12, Clark's ships hugged the shore of West Swanton and then sailed almost due north.

Their first objective was to strike at Caldwell's Manor, present-day Clarenceville, Quebec. The small village is on the northwest portion of Missisquoi Bay, just above Alburgh. About one hundred riflemen disembarked from their boats and plundered the community.[192] That Clark targeted this small town is not a surprise. Any contraband flowing north on the east side of the lake would have seeped through Caldwell's Manor and the surrounding tiny communities. The primary objective was Mr. Cook's store, where $300 worth of leather and shoes were seized. Clark believed this material had recently been smuggled and was on its way to the English army.

View from Missisquoi Bay, looking south into Lake Champlain. Isaac Clark's October 1813 raids originated from Burlington and Plattsburgh, to the south. *Photo by Armand Messier of northernvermontaerial.com.*

View looking north into Missisquoi Bay. Isaac Clark's raiding vessels traveled through this area to assault Canadian territory in October 1813. *Photo by Armand Messier of northernvermontaerial.com.*

View of the northernmost point of the Missisquoi River Delta. Clark's raiding ships passed by here in October 1813. *Photo by Armand Messier of northernvermontaerial.com.*

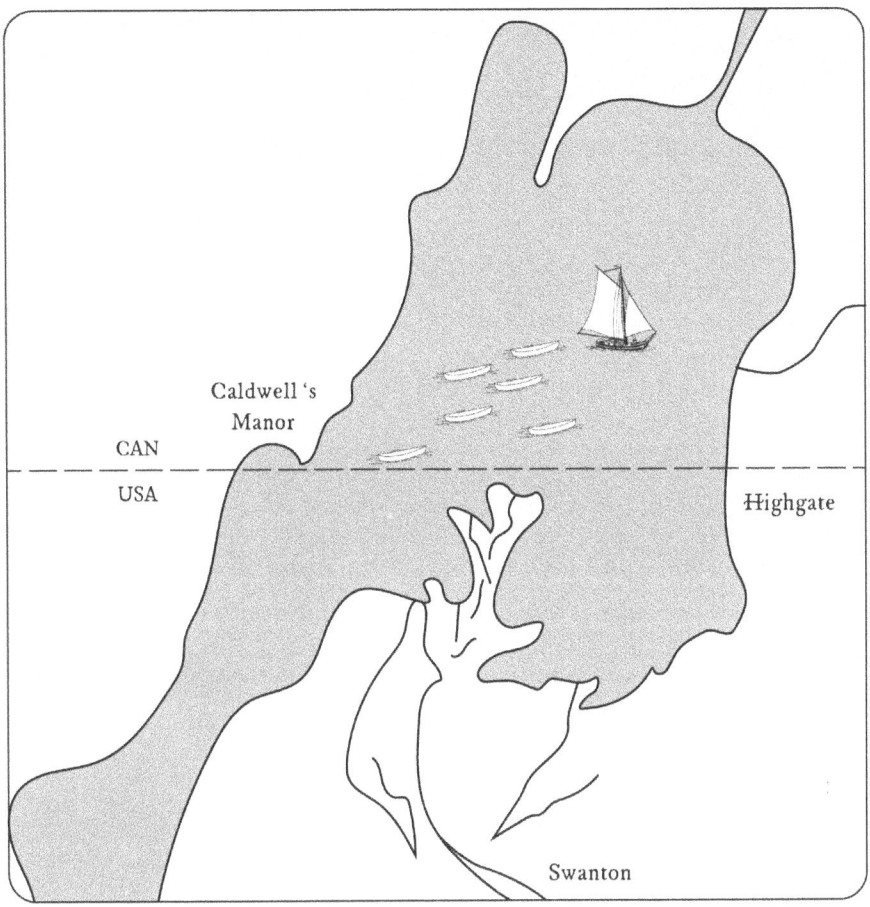

American fleet approaches the Canadian towns north of Highgate and Swanton. *Artwork by Lindsay DiDio.*

Clark and his men did not stay long in Caldwell's Manor. They moved eastward across the shallow waters of Missisquoi Bay and embarked toward the border towns. The bay is not terribly deep; generally, its depth is twelve to sixteen feet and grows progressively shallower near the shore of Highgate. The American bateaux approached swampy Rock River, in American territory, about a mile south of Quebec. The flotilla deposited the riflemen, a few militiamen and some small artillery.[193] They moved quietly through the woods of Highgate and crossed the border, attempting to avoid being noticed by Canadian or English pickets. The riflemen snuck north first, with the group of militia and the artillery bringing up the rear.[194] The sloop, scows and bateaux then moved slightly to the north, off the coast of Phillipsburg, Quebec, at about daybreak on the morning of October 12. If the raid went poorly from the start, the artillery from the boats would provide additional firepower. As word spread that the Americans had raided Caldwell's Manor and a Yankee flotilla was sailing in the bay, the Canadian militia roused and tried to organize.

Due to the land invasion underway by Wilkinson and Hampton, the Fourth Battalion, Select Embodied Militia of Lower Canada, was in the general area of the Canadian townships above the Vermont border.[195] Made up primarily of local farmers, the unit was ill-prepared. They mustered and attempted to confront the American force. Clark's men first encountered the advanced guard of the Canadian unit, under the command of Major Powell. Powell and this group were quickly captured, including the unit's leadership. The rest of the militia encountered Clark's 100-man landing party, and a brief battle ensued. According to Clark's report afterward, "Ten minutes after the first attack they laid down their arms and surrendered themselves prisoners of war."[196] A small number of Canadians were killed, 14 wounded, 101 taken prisoner. Reverend C.J. Stewart, the Anglican rector of Philipsburg and Frelighsburg, later wrote, "Early in the morning, about 150 men under the command of Colonel Clark attacked our militia at Philipsburg, Missisquoi Bay. This militia had been assembled there a few days before but at the time of the attack were only 100 strong and were not yet properly organized and armed."[197] The remaining elements of the Fourth Battalion attempted to deal with the crisis. To counter the invaders, 200 under the command of Lieutenant Colonel Luke organized to counter the invaders. Clark sent a small unit to probe Luke's forces and captured the Canadian scouts. The rest of the Canadian militia retreated at this point, unwilling to further test the Americans. The bulk of the American force, approximately 300 more men waiting in the bay, came ashore. The confiscation of smuggled goods, plundering of the local citizens and the effort to deny the English anything of value went into full swing. They took seventy-six firearms, confiscated the goods in two stores worth approximately $4,500 and drove off horses and oxen. One account noted, "Many marauding parties straggled from the troops, committed incessant robberies on the inhabitants contiguous to the Line, driving off their cattle, their horses, wagons, etc, and robbing the families of cloths, provisions, bedding, etc, to a very considerable amount."[198] A few Canadian families would later submit reports that, after the U.S. troops ransacked their homes, they were left with only the clothing on their backs.[199]

The value of hit-and-run raids was in the swiftness of their execution. Despite the success and the lack of casualties, remaining on the northern side of the border invited further confrontation. There is conflicting data on how the Canadian prisoners were removed from their homeland. Some sources have them marched down to Swanton, while Clark noted that he used the boats to get them out of Canadian territory.[200] Fully aware that Lieutenant Colonel Luke was still in the area with the remaining elements of the Fourth Battalion, perhaps as many as three hundred men, Clark withdrew from Canadian territory with his prisoners on October 12. His bateaux full of confiscated goods and his men encouraged by the success of their mission, the fleet departed Missisquoi Bay and returned to the safety of American waters. The benefits of parading the captured soldiers through the border towns was obvious. The U.S. Army could tout the success of a raid into enemy territory. The military probably wanted to send a message to the numerous smugglers in the area, too. The prisoners were marched south to Burlington, where a reporter from the *Boston Messenger* documented, "I have just seen Colonel Clark's prisoners, who were paraded through town. They are a motley crew of farmers, citizens, tavern-keepers, and traders, etc. not a regular soldier among them. They were surprised in their beds."

Clark's raid wasn't the last action of the fall, and the small-scale military activity intensified throughout October and November. Unsubstantiated reports emerged in the press that the British navy was operating inside of

View of Highgate, Vermont, looking east. *Photo by Armand Messier of northernvermontaerial.com.*

Missisquoi Bay. Clark's raiding fleet was about a mile north of this position in October 1813. *Photo by Armand Messier of northernvermontaerial.com.*

Missisquoi Bay and Canadian militia were raiding over the border.[201] Like a pot being brought from a simmer to a boil, the frequency of the incursions increased. Colonel Clark was very much a part of that activity.

About two weeks after the venture into Missisquoi Bay, Clark received information about a large herd of cattle destined to be smuggled over the border. He weighed the benefits of another strike and enlisted the help of the navy once again. The mission had two prongs, both making use of some of the smaller navy ships and the bateaux. He took command of a cavalry unit and proceeded across the lake to Grand Isle, then Swanton. While he organized his raid to retrieve the cattle, a company of riflemen packed in bateaux rowed north into Missisquoi Bay. They allowed themselves to be a distraction and once again took up a position on the east side of the bay, at the mouth of Rock River in Highgate, just a mile from the St. Armond border. While this feint was underway, Clark struck north with his small cavalry unit, galloping several miles into Quebec to the town of Frelighsburg.[202] The small community is just north of Huntsburgh, which was notorious for its role in the ongoing smuggling. Clark seized the cattle, and his company of horsemen escorted them back to Swanton. The riflemen stationed in Missisquoi Bay departed as well.[203]

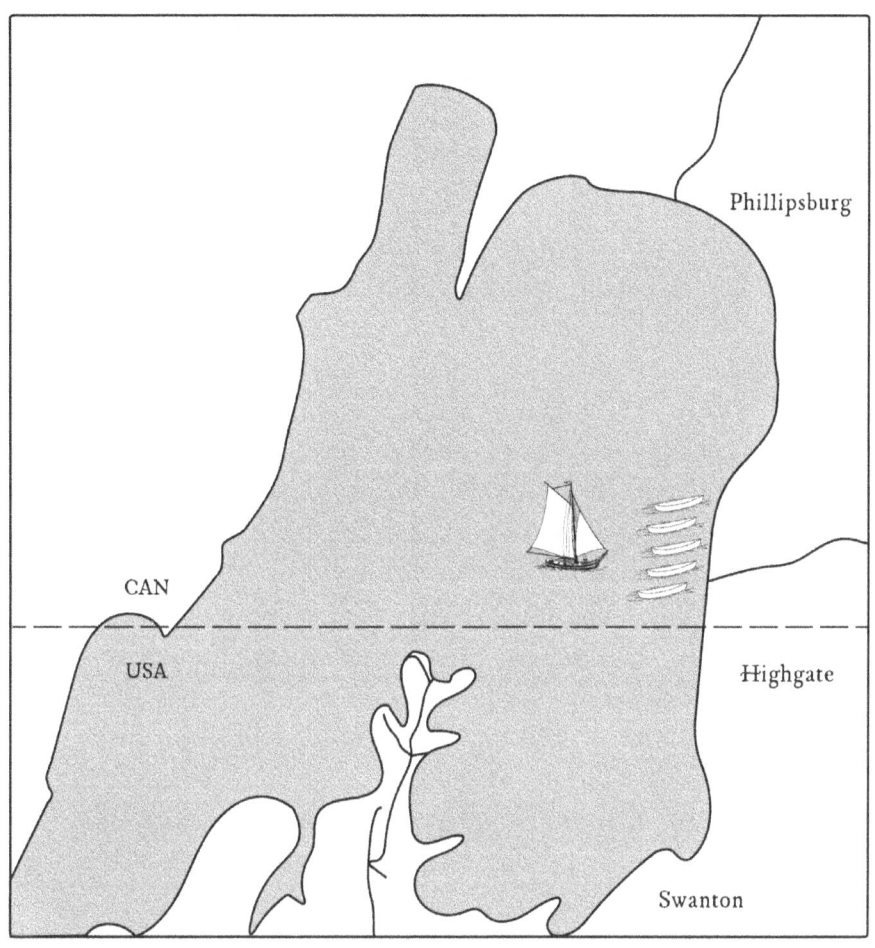

Isaac Clark returned to Missisquoi Bay for more raids later in October 1813. *Artwork by Lindsay DiDio.*

All of this activity was supposed to complement the other American invasion operating a little farther west in upstate New York. General Hampton's forces had moved up the Great Chazy River by bateaux in the last weeks of September. The four thousand men traveled as far as they could up the water route, and significant amounts of artillery and cavalry were brought up in support. After a small change in plans, Hampton embarked farther west to Chateaugay, New York. As the American army had tried to do during the fall of 1812, Hampton was determined to move against the smaller number of British and Canadian units blocking the shortest advance toward Montreal. Organization proved to be

View of Missisquoi Bay looking north. Isaac Clark's raiding forces were in this area in the fall of 1813. *Photo by Armand Messier of northernvermontaerial.com.*

Rock River in Highgate. Clark's second raiding party landed here in late October 1813. *Photo by Armand Messier of northernvermontaerial.com.*

a major problem, and while his army was in Chateaugay for nearly a month, another American army under General Wilkinson failed to make the planned rendezvous. Hampton's men watched the last of the prime weather of the fighting season slip away. The temperatures got colder, the leaves began to turn and still the two American armies remained apart. It wasn't until October 21 that the force finally got underway for Montreal. It eventually suffered the same fate as the other attempted invasions but marked the most significant American push yet into Canadian territory.

Unlike the previous attempts, this one at least moved a significant distance into Canada. The advance came to an end when a much smaller force of Canadian militia, British regulars and groups of Indians placed themselves on the north banks of the Chateaugay River. Their defensive positions were enough to turn back the Americans. They did so by conducting an amazingly loud defense, exaggerating their troop strength every single time units were deployed. General Hampton was fooled into thinking he was up against a much larger force. The Americans gave up on that attempt, but Wilkinson's army to the west suffered a similar fate. His army of over two thousand men was halted by about eight hundred defenders at the battle of Chrysler's Farm.[204] The communication between the two American forces was so poor Hampton was removed from command and portions of his army started back for Plattsburgh and Burlington. It is important to keep note of the movements of the larger forces, because the events in Vermont would often revolve around what was unfolding not so far to the west.

American naval activity on Lake Champlain increased as MacDonough brought yet another four vessels into service by the end of October. Joining his sloops, scows and assorted vessels moving back and forth between Burlington, Plattsburgh and Missisquoi Bay were new gunboats. The gunboats under MacDonough's command were christened *Ludlow*, *Wilmer*, *Alwyn* and *Ballard*.

Meanwhile, the British did what they could to stab back at the Americans and inserted themselves into U.S. territory multiple times both on and off the lake. While Vermont land east of Missisquoi Bay remained virtually ignored by the British, the New York communities across the lake were not as lucky. Pliny Moore, a resident of the area, recorded the British incursions in his journal.[205] He described an incursion on October 28 where three hundred soldiers under the command of Major Perrault entered Champlain. They returned on November 2 with nearly one thousand soldiers and plundered the homes of American citizens.

On November 3, the British left Isle Aux Noix, crossed the border with four gunboats and waited for a small incursion by the British army to destroy American supplies in Chazy, New York. When the land attack never materialized, the gunboats took matters into their own hands, traveled to Windmill Point in Alburgh and destroyed the customshouse and other government buildings there. Interested in making sure the entrance to the Richelieu River was defended, the lightly armed British sloop *Canada* was deployed between Ash Island and the mouth of the Richelieu River as a patrol vessel. They had taken note of the increased American activity and were trying to give Isle Aux Noix advanced notice of any threats.[206]

Not content to just let the threats emerge, the British set out again to harass upstate New York. Pliny Moore's journal notes that fifty enemy cavalrymen descended across the line on November 14. They remained until the sixteenth.[207] On the seventeenth, the gunboats emerged and were there to support a landing at Chazy, New York. When the operation was complete, and there was no immediate response from the Americans, the gunboats proceeded south the next day. They went to Isle La Motte before heading back to the safety of the Richelieu River.

During November, American customs agents worked in concert with the navy in Missisquoi Bay. MacDonough and the sloop *President*, along with the smaller government customs vessel *Alert*, moved into the waters near the line. They seized a smuggling vessel that carried furs and dry goods.[208]

Falling temperatures alone are not enough to restrict the movement of an army. Foot soldiers and horsemen can still maneuver over frozen ground. The lake is a different story, and operating vessels in late fall became problematic for both sides. Temperatures generally fell well below freezing during the night and caused difficulty for the men deployed on the water. The lake and the extreme southern edge of the Richelieu River are generally at their lowest levels just before the water freezes, forcing some of the larger vessels to avoid shallow water. The arrival of the cold and the expansion of ice over the water puts a complete halt to naval activity. Still, the British were able to send ships far enough south on December 4 to reach Cumberland Head near Plattsburgh, where they successfully torched a storehouse.[209] Four American vessels were ordered to confront the raiding craft, but the British retreated. A three-hour chase ensued, but it ended when the British ships returned to the narrows of the Richelieu. Having learned their lesson in June, the Americans refused to continue their pursuit. This would be the conclusion of naval activity on the lake for a few months. The British set their vessels into winter quarters during the middle of December. MacDonough brought his fleet down to Burlington by December 21. While the fleets were now inactive, both sides were committing unprecedented resources to control the waters of Lake Champlain.

10

SPHERES OF INFLUENCE

Winter 1813–1814

For the most part, the War of 1812 is remembered much more fondly north of the border than to the south. American history is full of war and conflict, and many of the incidents are portrayed with a patriotic slant in which the United States defeats a large foreign power or saves other countries from tyranny. The embarrassing failures of the War of 1812 often don't fit on the same pages as conquests and victories.

The War of 1812 represents exactly that to Canada. Considering the stature that its neighbor to the south later attained, an area where aggressive American armies suffered failure at the hands of vastly inferior forces—well, that deserves notoriety. The winter of 1813 and 1814 represents such a time. American armies massed on the New York border and marched toward Montreal on multiple occasions. They were stopped each time. Any Canadian historian who dwells on these facts as a matter of national pride rightly does so. The American efforts were so inept that some don't even reach the status of full-blown invasions. Considering the overall effort was to seize Montreal and blunt England's ability to wage war on the continent, Canada has the right to more than a little national pride.

The persistent raiding between the two sides didn't stop with the arrival of a new season. In fact, the arrival of winter marked a distinct uptick in activity, with the short-term advantage going to the Crown. Much of that has to do with what played out directly after the Christmas of 1813.[210]

The small barracks and cantonment that the U.S. government had maintained for more than a year in Derby grabbed the attention of the

British. During the winter of 1812–13 it had been used to house three companies of the Edward Fifield's Vermont militia. The primary goal had always been to patrol the border and prevent smuggling. However, the possibility always existed that the federal government would try to repeat Benedict Arnold's brave efforts of 1776 and launch an invasion of Quebec through the dense wilderness of northern New England. The two sides were in the midst of hitting any target they could along the border, and the Americans had made the mistake, as in Swanton, of leaving the Derby barracks virtually undefended.

The area had a similar dynamic to the towns on Lake Champlain. Large numbers of Vermonters in the Northeast Kingdom traded beef and other products to the north. Militia participation did not prevent citizens from engaging in questionable activities.[211] On December 27, a small number of British troops working with detachments of Canadian militia crossed the border near Lake Memphremagog.[212] The raiders may have carried off a large amount of the American supplies.[213]

The militia presence in Derby was centered on the barracks and supply buildings, built at some point during the late summer and fall of 1812. The small military installation was located near Hinman Pond, near where several local roads intersect just south of the line.[214]

Its proximity to the border made the outpost a prime target. British captain Oliver Barker, some of his direct subordinates and members of the Stanstead County militia of Quebec carried out the raid.[215] With Isaac Clark raiding all the way into Frelighsburg only a month and a half before, it is understandable why the local militia were eager to participate in action against the Americans. The network of smugglers provided the British and Canadians with good intelligence. They rode their horses over the border, entered the village of Derby and approached the barracks. Soldiers, with their rifles drawn, scouted the surrounding area and kept locals at bay. When small amounts of supplies, ammunition and arms were discovered, the raiders looted what they could. After the raid, in reports to their commanders, the British specifically noted members of the Stanstead County militia who helped in the raid. Captains Curtis and Taplin, Lieutenants Messa and Bodwell and Ensign Boynton were the most involved, but many militia members were present.[216] The barracks and supply building were torched, and then the British and Canadians went home. Warfare now engulfed nearly the entire Quebec-Vermont border.

Another small raid was conducted against an American patrol along the line in January. British intelligence received word that squads of

Americans were moving in and out of the woods along farmland in Highgate. Still stinging from Clark's raids and buoyed by the success of the attack on Derby, local militiamen organized and prepared to ambush the American dragoons. The small incident went well for the Canadians, who killed one enemy soldier, severely wounded two others and took six prisoners.[217]

The most significant military activities were the preparations for the next sailing season on Lake Champlain. The incidents along the border were not key to who would end up controlling the lake. Both sides began a massive investment in trying to build bigger and better ships capable of outdoing anything the other side could produce.

For the British, central to that activity was Isle Aux Noix, which once again experienced exponential growth and activity. In February, MacDonough attempted to gather intelligence about what the British were up to.[218] The information was not extensive, but they became aware that the naval yard at Isle Aux Noix had been upgraded and the British were in the process of constructing a very large vessel. What the British were building was the hull of the brig *Linnet*. It was to be eighty-five feet long and could carry more guns than anything presently in the American fleet.

The Americans had moved their shipbuilding efforts south, farther away from any British incursions, so that work would remain uninterrupted. MacDonough had settled into Vergennes, Vermont, as his new headquarters and celebrated the benefits of his new location. First, with the physical barrier of ice covering the lake, any effort by the British to collect intelligence was reliant on spies alone. The agents would be heavily exposed. The more in the open they were, the greater the chance the military could find and eliminate them.

There were other benefits to Vergennes. The local economy was strong enough that MacDonough relied on existing industry. Vast areas of oak and pine trees needed for the construction of larger naval vessels populated the surrounding areas. Sawmills, more than a half-dozen forges, two already existing furnaces, a rolling mill and a wire factory were already operating on the banks of Otter Creek. Communication wouldn't be an encumbrance, as fine roads existed to Burlington and other points farther south in New England.[219] When MacDonough received intelligence that the British were building the larger vessel, it didn't take him long to recognize that it might pulverize *Preble*, *Montgomery*, *Frances*, *Wasp*, *President* and his collection of gunboats and scows. While he had shown a certain amount of magic in converting small and mid-sized commercial sailing vessels into serviceable military craft, a true military sailing vessel would be more than a match for his hodge-podge fleet.

The navy understood the situation and gave MacDonough options for what he could build to counter the British. Approval for four more gunboats was granted, and the navy agreed to invest in a true military sailing ship of its own. Plans were approved for the construction of a large sailing vessel. Work began on converting the hull of the steamer—the "transport" vessel the army had originally loaned him in the fall of 1812—into a warship. Construction crews, carpenters and the appropriate number of seamen were desperately assembled, and work began at a furious pace.

Meanwhile, the American army leadership refused to give up on resuming the offensive. Isle Aux Noix, located so tantalizingly close in the confines of the Richelieu, always seemed like an insect that the American military could not swipe away. Since it was the closest installation in any invasion targeting Montreal, it had to be dealt with.

The American decision to proceed doesn't seem as foolhardy as one might think. If the army was properly fitted with winter gear, the trek north was not impossible. Something had to be attempted, sooner rather than later. The situation in Europe was changing rapidly for the British, and if troops were freed up from their fight with Napoleon, it was a foregone conclusion that reinforcements would be sent to defend Canada. Finally, the state of the army was vastly better than it had been in the fall of 1812. It was strong enough that it no longer had to rely on the militia, who grumbled and stumbled getting to the border and then refused to go north when they got there. So, plans were put together for yet another American thrust north.

After completing other attempts in western New York that yielded no results, focus once again fell to the Champlain Valley. Any sick and injured troops were deposited in the Burlington hospital, where conditions were considerably better than they had been just twelve months before. Dr. Mann worked in Burlington and dealt with a flare-up of some of the same diseases that plagued the area in the winter of 1812. Burlington was organized and sanitary enough to deal with it effectively this time. When hundreds died during the previous cold season, ninety-five deaths were recorded during the winter of 1813.[220] The sick still numbered in the hundreds, but far fewer were dying.

General Wilkinson, frustrated that the activity in the fall did not provide results, began to organize his forces. In January, he ordered cavalry stationed in Burlington to proceed across the frozen lake where they combined with dragoons arriving from French Mills, New York. With the decision to move north reached, Wilkinson wanted as solid intelligence as he could get and ordered his rangers to report on the situation at Isle Aux Noix. With these movements also came a series of deployments along the New York frontier, effectively giving the British the impression that the American army could cross the border wherever it wanted to.[221]

The best accounts of what was about to transpire come from the soldiers themselves. Colonel George McFeely of the Twenty-Fifth Infantry regiment detailed his experiences in his diary. Throughout January and February, he reported that it was "exceedingly" cold and in some areas the snow approached four feet deep. On some nights, the soldiers had to make temporary shanties with hemlock boughs.[222] Once Wilkinson had made his decision, Colonel McFeely's men were ordered to Plattsburgh, where they arrived in late January. During the trek from Four Corners and Chateaugay, the snow caused a lot of trouble for the army on the move.

Arriving in the last days of January, his soldiers were able to enjoy the rough comforts of the city while the rest of the American army was brought into place. When his soldiers were sent to patrol the lines north of Plattsburgh in early February, the temperature fell again, with at least one night reaching thirty below zero. He noted that many of his men were falling ill from exposure to the elements.

Like the weather, military plans can always be in flux, and General Wilkinson fell prey to temporarily exploring the idea of moving the invasion back to the west, once again trying to bring the American army up through the St. Lawrence, just south of Montreal. McFeely, his men and other units were ordered west once more but then returned to Plattsburgh by February 21. After exposure to the frigid Northeast winter, with no productive engagements against the enemy, one can see why morale was low. Finally, Wilkinson decided on his thrust northward, along the western shore of Lake Champlain. He had most of his army in Plattsburgh, where the invasion could commence.[223] He sent General Macomb, with the Sixth and Fifteenth Regiments, to Burlington. The details were being worked out, but northern Vermont was about to get yet another healthy dose of what war was like.

Of note once again is Sheldon resident Frances Duclos, who had been aiding smugglers and feeding information to the British. In this instance, he was able to gather intelligence about planned American troop movements and raids into Caldwell's Manor and other Quebec communities.[224] As the military deployment in Vermont grew, citizens with divided loyalties were like sly foxes, never wanting to be seen, but willing to steal whatever they could. Information sent by Duclos made it to Isle Aux Noix.

With McFeely and his soldiers in Plattsburgh, and other elements of the army finally arriving in force, they once again received orders to embark, but this time for Vermont. On February 27, they marched across the frozen lake and arrived in Burlington, where his unit was woven into General Macomb's Brigade. Nathan Haswell, helping to organize the supplies for the army, noted the rations at the time. Each soldier was given around a pound of pork or beef, a little more than a pound of bread and some whiskey, brandy or rum.[225]

Colonel Clark was already back in Swanton by March 12, with elements of his Eleventh Regiment, having been wrapped into the command staff of General Macomb's brigade. Clark was about to be the eyes and ears of the much larger force. While patrolling the border, his men had already seized twenty-three sleigh loads of goods destined for Canada.[226] As the middle of March arrived, he prepared to make another dash across the border. The need to crush the smuggling carried an added urgency at this point. Anything being smuggled so close to the British fortifications at Isle Aux Nois were likely destined for that location.

As the regiments stationed in Burlington were departing for Swanton, Wilkinson had brought up the main portion of his army from Plattsburgh to the Canadian border. Many historians portray Wilkinson as having a grandiose sense of elevated self-importance. They note that he believed he was leading a campaign that would be linked with the grand Napoleonic Wars of Europe or the campaigns from the French and Indian Wars.[227] Wilkinson, more than any other general in the theater, had finally come up with a strategy to seize the thorn in the side of the American forces since the start of the war. While it took him months, he'd come to understand that a thrust against Montreal through the Champlain Valley needed to be carried out, and that Isle Aux Noix had to be the first target in that campaign.

Situational realities may have also come into play. With MacDonough busily constructing his fleet down in Otter Creek, the rumors that the British were getting close to completing the brig *Linnet* started to spread. Speculation that they would accelerate their now-established shipbuilding at Isle Aux Noix was a great concern at the top levels of command. If they could finish the *Linnet* in just a few months, what was next? If the British naval yard just a few miles north of the border remained untouched, the American navy on Lake Champlain might not be able to compete. The planning was also more deliberate, and for the first time, the Americans were engaged in a serious thrust to attack the island.

By March 15, Colonel Clark had received more men in Swanton and had pushed north. The invasion was to be a two-pronged effort, like fingers coming together to squeeze from two sides. The main portion of the invasion, Wilkinson's large force just south of the border in northern New York, waited to see the results of Clark's and Macomb's move north from Vermont. Clark had approximately six hundred men with him and moved his forces about two miles east of Missisquoi Bay.[228] He wrote to Macomb, requesting the rest of the brigade be brought up in support.

For the first and only time during the War of 1812, Swanton and the northern Vermont communities were the launching point for an invasion. At least as planned, it wasn't supposed to be a raid or quick thrust across the border. Wilkinson was supposed to attack Isle Aux Noix from the southwest. Clark and Macomb were already threatening from the Vermont side.

Events in war are random and always changing, though.

II
A HUB ONCE AGAIN

Spring 1814

Isaac Clark was left waiting, a bit exposed, just after he crossed the Canadian line. The fog of war makes the troop movements of one's enemy difficult to predict. Isle Aux Noix was just a few short miles away, and he could not know how the enemy would react. He didn't even know if his left flank, which was tucked up against the frozen waters of Missisquoi Bay, was secure. It was possible the enemy could strike from the ice. After all, American units had marched over the ice just days before.

Clark, who had shown a history for aggressive action over the last two years, especially with his knowledge of the region, didn't hedge. He ordered his soldiers to inch farther north.

His anxiety was tempered by the arrival of more men. Colonel McFeely's journal provides more information about the movement of his own troops and other support units. He wrote that the Fifteenth, Sixteenth and his own unit, the Twenty-Second Regiment, had moved north from Burlington on March 18. His account is short but detailed. The roads were very bad, causing some of the supplies and equipment to be delayed.[229] They arrived in Swanton, with General Macomb, on March 20.

By March 22, Clark occupied Phillipsburg again, but this time with a much larger force.[230] During the initial movement over the border, Clark wrote to personal ally Senator Robinson and updated him on the progress of the incursion.[231] Clark's concern about being exposed was alleviated when no elements of the Canadian militia moved to oppose him. The arrival of General Macomb's eight hundred infantrymen, an additional three

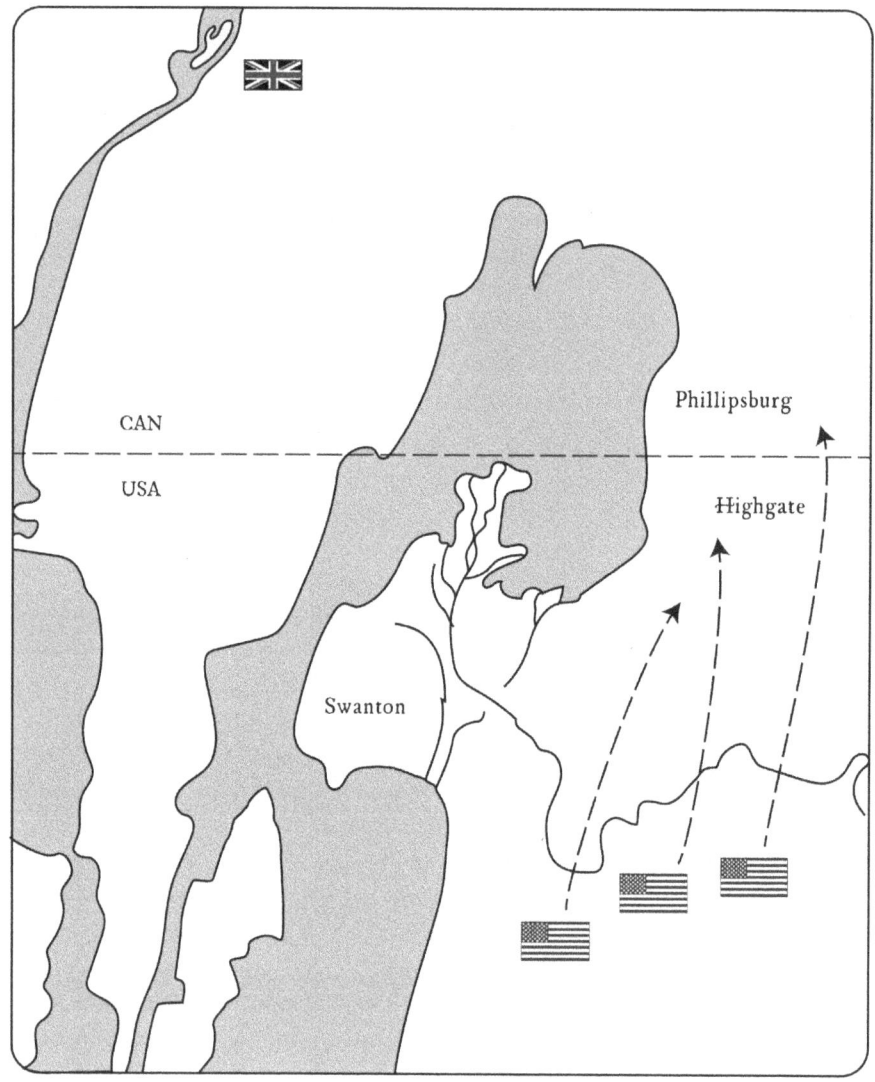

March 1814. American army once again returns to the Quebec border towns. *Artwork by Lindsay DiDio.*

regiments with eight pieces of artillery, gave him still more confidence.[232] The units touched on in Colonel McFeely's diary were part of this force.

Meanwhile, across the lake, final preparations were made to cross the border. Wilkinson had about 3,200 men as the main force of his army and was on the doorstep of the enemy. The general waffled as to if he should take out Isle Aux Noix or bypass the island and threaten Montreal. In these critical days and hours of late March, deficiencies in American leadership once again caused hesitation and the eventual disintegration of a campaign before it even started. Wilkinson wanted information about how strong the ice was on the Richelieu River, particularly in the area surrounding the British fortifications, so he ordered scouting missions from the occupying forces in Phillipsburg.

The indecision that gripped Wilkinson suddenly spread to the force deployed north of Swanton. In enemy territory, so close to their objective but without orders to attack, Macomb, Clark's and McFeely's men were forced to wait for days. Colonel Clark ordered his men to do what they had done multiple times before, search private homes and businesses for items that had been smuggled from the United States. While his intent was no different than it had ever been, it caused tension in the ranks. Macomb believed Clark's men were looting the homes of private citizens. McFeely, caught in the middle of the uninspiring breakdown of the command structure, noted the events in his journal. Clark produced his earlier communications with the customs officers and described the orders that led to his earlier missions. Macomb essentially accused his men of plunder and robbery. The arguments worsened, with Macomb threatening to have Clark arrested on the spot. Then Clark, who had somehow remained healthy throughout the botched campaigns and epidemics of disease over the previous winters, took ill. He became so sick he was bedridden. McFeely feared Macomb would order Clark arrested while sick in bed.[233]

Circumstances forced the squabbling American commanders to reorient themselves. Wilkinson, suddenly convinced that he should have all his army in one place for the assault, ordered Macomb's entire brigade to cease activity near Missisquoi Bay and rejoin his forces in New York. While these orders were being carried out on the night of March 25, with the Americans giving up their position in Phillipsburg, the Canadian militia moved in. The British and Canadians had been unwilling to take the bait and engage in a winter land battle, but they were perfectly fine with harassing an indecisive enemy.

On the morning of March 26, the Canadian militia, aware that most of Macomb's brigade was filtering south, engaged the northernmost pickets. The outnumbered Canadians fired at a house where an American squad had spent the night. The American companies sent to reinforce the northern pickets were unable to engage the suspected four hundred Canadian militia, who had moved off to the northwest. Seeing the last chances for an engagement evaporate, McFeely joined the rest of Macomb's brigade to the south. They moved through worsening weather all day, back across the line into Highgate and camped in Swanton on the evening of the twenty-sixth. It rained heavily all night. Wilkinson finally settled on an initial attack against the enemy positions in Lacolle Mills.[234] On March 27, Macomb ordered his forces to move over the slushy ice-covered waters of Missisquoi Bay, to join Wilkinson's army near the town of Champlain.[235]

The reasons for Wilkinson's shift in strategy are unclear, but his approach was grounded in the intelligence reports coming out of Canada. Despite the winter, the shipbuilding facilities at Isle Aux Noix had ramped up considerably. Scouts reported that the brig *Linnet* was nearing completion. Unknown to the Americans, construction of more, larger gunboats was about to start.[236]

Wilkinson's indecisiveness cost the Americans their final opportunity to attack Isle Aux Noix from two directions on March 27. Macomb's Brigade had camped the night in Alburgh and, given that town's unique geography, could have been the staging area for a quick strike north. While it would not have divided the enemy, as the aborted attack from Missisquoi Bay could have, it still offered a chance to confuse the British and Canadians, to throw the fog of war onto the campaign. From Alburgh, the American units could have been at Isle Aux Noix's doorstep in half a day. Wilkinson wavered again and returned to his original thinking, that the attack would take place through northern New York.

Before doing so, a small element of Macomb's Brigade was ordered back east, all the way to Lake Memphremagog. As his own invasion of Quebec neared, Wilkinson thought it best a few companies be in the general area where the barracks had been burned just three months ago, near Derby. In total, about 250 infantrymen were on their way to Barton, Vermont.[237]

For those joining Wilkinson's invasion, the night of the twenty-seventh was an unforgiving one. Macomb's Brigade, losing daylight in Alburgh, spent the night in the open with no tents. The men huddled near open fires to stay warm, but the frigid winds had increased substantially.[238]

With most of his army now together, Wilkinson ordered more scouting, trying to determine which of three routes to use to attack Lacolle Mills.[239] However, the weather had turned, and even many of his subordinates were losing faith in the idea of an immediate attack. Macomb's Brigade had moved across the lake from Alburgh to Rouses Point on the morning of the twenty-eighth and encountered treacherous conditions. The recent rains had made the march from Swanton slushy and difficult, as the precipitation had frozen. There was now a sheet of slick surface ice over the narrows of the lake. Colonel McFeely wrote in his diary on the twenty-eighth that it was "slick as glass" and that several soldiers lost their footing. During falls, some men cut themselves on other soldiers' bayonets. Still others suffered separated shoulders.[240]

With the army together, Wilkinson ordered it over the border on March 30. They immediately encountered felled trees over roads, and horses became exhausted in the deep snow. The attack went as poorly as previous invasion attempts and was over quickly. The firing started at Odelltown and involved a skirmish where the British and Canadian militia took advantage of the bad weather. The Americans had difficulty bringing up their artillery in the snow. The tiny British contingent opened fire on the exposed artillerymen but quickly withdrew when American infantry units were brought up in support.[241] Most of the American army was unable to get into position until later in the afternoon. The attack did progress, more intensely than in the fall of 1812, and it did have a greater chance for success. Wilkinson deployed the whole of his army and launched a large attack at the Lacolle Stone Mill, where only two hundred Canadians and English soldiers defended. Flanking maneuvers were made, and for a time, it seemed the enemy might abandon their position.[242] British reserves were rushed to the battle from Isle Aux Noix, and the number of defenders along the north bank of the LaColle River increased to close to one thousand men. Americans continued to approach, but the fire was withering and the attack faltered. Wilkinson ordered sergeants to shoot any man deserting from the battlefield.[243] The enemy's defensive position was solidly anchored along the rise of the riverbank, the stone mill and the blockhouse. Further reinforcements came with the arrival of British naval support on the Richelieu. The soldiers at Isle Aux Noix had been breaking the ice around the fort all winter, just for this very contingency. When the firing started, the sloop *Broke* and a few of the gunboats took up a position where the Sorel River flows into the Richelieu, just east of the mill. The vessels anchored at the exposed flank of the defenders. Needed supplies and small cannons were sent from the ships to the stone mill to aid in its defense.[244]

In the vicinity of the mill, Wilkinson's forces vastly outnumbered the defenders, but he was unwilling to order a charge. The attack came to an end, and he ordered his grand army to withdraw south. The casualties for both sides eclipsed anything experienced by either side to that point along the northern border. Everything had been raids, skirmishes and quick strikes. Ships or property had always been seized or destroyed, but the loss of life had never been terribly notable. That changed with Wilkinson's failed attack on the mill. The British casualties were: 10 men had died, 46 were wounded and 4 soldiers were missing. But they had held their ground. American casualties were much higher. The entire effort had wasted time, provided another defeat and led to painful casualty numbers: 13 men were dead, 128 were wounded and 13 were missing.

The invasion force retreated across the border and attempted to lick its wounds. Wilkinson was removed from command by the War Department. General Macomb was promoted and would share oversight of the theater with General Izard, who was set to arrive later.

The failure of the Americans to launch any sort of sustained threat against Montreal became doubly important at that point. On the very same days that Wilkinson's invasion petered out, Napoleon was defeated in France. Allied European armies had approached Paris in late March, and Napoleon surrendered on March 31. With France temporarily defeated and no longer a drain on resources, England could take the opportunity to reinforce its position in the Americas. Quebec City and Montreal were the ports where those men would land on the American continent. With so many resources now free, the British turned more of their attention to the United States. It would only be a few months before the size of their army in Canada increased substantially.

On April 6, Peter Sailly, writing to MacDonough from Plattsburgh, reported that once the ice had gone out, British ships had been between Rouses Point and Alburgh several times. Sailly also forwarded intelligence that the British might try to block the entrance to Otter Creek, essentially preventing the American squadron from ever seeing the lake. He noted that they might sink sloops filled with stones at the mouth of Otter Creek.[245] About a month later, the British inched onto the lake, flexing newfound superiority. The *Linnet* was finished, and with its arrival they could venture south with the firepower to back it up.

With new American ships nearing completion, and spring softening the ground enough for work to begin on defending Vergennes, the army constructed defensive positions at the head of Otter Creek. The site would be named Fort Cassen, after McDonough's second in command. The effort was a hastily-put-together, makeshift trench, along with a few naval carriages.[246] The army and navy cobbled together seven twelve-pound cannons, pointing them north and west in the event the British sailed the lake from Isle Aux Noix. A regiment of Vermont militia was also called out after the generals convinced the governor that an attack was coming. About five hundred militiamen were sent to Burlington to protect the harbor against any landing, and nearly one thousand were sent to guard the shipbuilding facilities at Vergennes.[247] It was another month before the British attempted to hit MacDonough.

On May 9, the English command sent Daniel Pring with the new *Linnet* south toward Alburgh and Rouses Point. *Linnet* had a substantial number of support ships. Four sloops (two of them formerly the *Broke* and *Shannon*)—the *Chub*, *Finch*, *Icicle* and *Canada*—and thirteen gunboats crossed into American waters.[248] Their first act was to seize a small schooner at Rouses Point, a ship that the U.S. Customs officials had just detained. The vessel was taken and sent north to Isle Aux Noix.[249] Word spread throughout the valley quickly, and General Izard promptly sent notification to Macomb in Burlington. Macomb informed MacDonough in Vergennes as the British sailed south. Fifty artillerymen from Burlington were sent by wagon to Vergennes to man the new defensive positions. The preparations were very real now that the enemy was coming.

It was a slower descent than Pring would have liked, having to deal with a stiff south wind and the arrival of rain. On May 10, his armada had barely made it past Cumberland Head. Reports spread that the English were seizing or destroying every boat they could find on the lake. They pursued a small customs boat into the shallow waters off Grand Isle, took the ferryboat that operated in that area and plundered the home of Mr. Bell, the operator of the ferry. They were going after every small craft within their grasp, attempting to eliminate the enemy's ability to move resources between Burlington and Plattsburgh. In one instance, they even took a private canoe.[250] At one point a gunboat pursued a smaller boat into the mouth of the Bouquet River, on the New York side. While there, they plundered a private home.[251]

While these small actions were part of a larger plan, Pring had not yet come close to achieving the mission objectives. Between May 10 and May 13, his fleet dominated the central portion of the lake. Before approaching Vergennes, they anchored off Providence Island and interrogated men unfortunate enough to be caught in a boat near his invasion fleet. He collected significant intelligence about MacDonough's work and the status of the two likely additions to the American fleet.[252] Pring now had firsthand knowledge that the *Saratoga* neared completion and the *Ticonderoga* wasn't far behind. He had to act if he was going to prevent those vessels from leaving the confines of Otter Creek.

On May 14, Pring brought his fleet into position to see what could be done against the Americans defending the mouth of Otter Creek. The attack was led by the *Linnet*, which moved into an area two and a half miles off the shore. Some of the gunboats began firing on the Americans occupying defensive embankments. And so, the brief Battle of Fort Cassen began.[253] The initial plan called for the gunboats to approach the shore and then storm the American defensive positions with Marines.

The landing was unable to happen due to the intensity of the fire from Fort Cassen and the presence of Vermont militia stationed in the woods on both sides of Otter Creek.[254] *Linnet* and the other vessels continued maneuvers and fired on the shore for about two hours. The American intelligence from a month earlier had proven correct: the British had intended to use the hulls of the *Icicle* and the *Canada* to obstruct Otter Creek. If they were sailed into the narrow mouth of the river and sunk, they would have bottled up MacDonough's new vessels farther inland. Due to the intensity of the barrage from Fort Cassen, Pring's ships were unable to get close enough. Rather than lose or damage his squadron, Pring ordered his forces back toward the border.

On the way north, two gunboats were sent in support of the one that had entered the Bouquet River the day before. Their quick mission was to destroy any public stores of flour used by the military. The Essex County militia was called out and engaged in an intense but brief firefight with one of the crews of the gunboats.[255] The fire from the militia was so effective that one of the British sloops was ordered into the mouth of the river to help tow away a gunboat after it was damaged.[256] The most important outcome of the effort was that Pring now had solid intelligence about MacDonough's ability to bring new vessels to the lake.

British ships were still on the lake and in American waters later in May, and they knew that MacDonough was on the verge of launching his fleet, so they did not venture south of Burlington. At least two British gunboats settled off the coast of Grand Ise on May 20. They had significant reason to harass shipping along the line and keep the Americans away from Isle Aux Noix. There, with knowledge of what the Americans had been working on, the first plans were developed for yet another sailing vessel, one that could compete with the ever-growing American presence. The plans called for a massive 147-foot, 37-gun ship.[257] So the harassment to the south continued, and in late May, private vessels in the vicinity of Plattsburgh and Burlington refused to go out on the lake with enemy vessels prowling so far below the line.[258]

Everything changed when MacDonough brought his entire squadron out of Vergennes, with a few of the vessels entirely new to Lake Champlain. His shipbuilders had completed refitting the steamship, and it was now a sixteen-gun schooner with two masts, the *Ticonderoga*. Returning to the fleet were the sloops from the previous season: *President*, now with ten guns, *Preble* with nine and *Montgomery* with six. The *Frances* and *Wasp*, the two private sloops that had been hastily armed and refitted after the events of Murray's Raid in August, were poor sailing vessels. Their guns were redistributed to the other vessels in the fleet and the ships returned to their owners. The last of the smaller vessels were the six new gunboats, each with two cannons. The Americans now had the most impressive vessel on the lake, one that could compete with *Linnet*. It was the twenty-six-gun *Saratoga*. On May 26, MacDonough's new flotilla was ready, and if the British would stay on the lake, he would confront them. The *Saratoga* was perhaps named as a historical reminder to the British, who had invaded the Champlain Valley during the Revolutionary War and lost their army at the Battle of Saratoga in 1777.

Thus begins one of the least patriotic periods in the history of the state of Vermont. History has not been critical enough of those who continued to engage in smuggling in the late spring and summer of 1814. Up to that point, it had been with an enemy almost always on the defensive in the Champlain Valley. The gravity of war profiteering was about to have much larger implications.

Indications that the British were preparing their own large-scale descent into the valley became apparent to the public with stories of the new vessel being constructed at Isle Aux Noix. If the British were able to deploy such a vessel, a lot of Americans would die in the fighting. Those involved in the smuggling failed to consider the long-term consequences if the British were able to win the war. Too many Vermonters continued to covertly help the English and Canadians, despite a British invasion of their homeland becoming more and more likely as spring melted into summer.

Across the ocean, orders were being put in place for a significant military buildup in the Americas. The British planned offensive operations on the East Coast of the United States, with a main invasion directly through the Champlain Valley.[259]

What the British were building at Isle Aux Noix was so massive that it could not be completed without traded goods from the Americans. It was to be the *Confiance*, a vessel so large it would equal the power of true oceangoing vessels within the British navy. In early June, MacDonough became aware of smuggling efforts in the northern part of the lake, specifically linked to the construction of the *Confiance*. In this specific instance, wood for the masts of the British ship was seized.[260] Ironically, the disloyal behavior increased the closer *Confiance* got to completion.

There was a flurry of activity on both sides of the border. If the British were going to push south, American defensive positions had to be prepared. At one point, the generals considered using the infantry to push a few miles into Canada and set up an artillery position on the south bank of the LaColle River. This plan was ambitious, allowing the Americans to fire on any British craft well before approaching Lake Champlain. But the effort was deemed too costly and the idea was abandoned. Rouses Point, just west of Alburgh, was also considered for a large artillery battery, but the terrain was judged too difficult and did not provide enough of an advantage. Eventually American engineers began working on defensive positions on Cumberland Head, just north of Plattsburgh.[261] The British increased their own defensive positions north of the border by adding two blockhouses on the Richelieu, improving the defensive networks near LaColle and strengthening their forward base on Ash Island. This work made it extremely difficult for American vessels to move north and interfere with their plans.

MacDonough knew he could not let the construction of the *Confiance* go unchecked, so he asked for permission to construct another vessel. The proposal was approved, and the shipbuilders at Vergennes prepared for the next phase of the arms race with their rivals at Isle Aux Noix.

Finally, the American fleet was brought into position where it could perform two duties. It needed to patrol and confront the British at the northern end of the lake, but some of the fleet was devoted to patrolling the waters for contraband. The American presence was so strong that orders were given in late spring and into the summer for the British ships bottled up on the Richelieu to not go any farther south than Windmill Point.[262] They didn't want to risk an engagement without superiority, and work on *Confiance* was underway.

12

VERMONT TO THE RESCUE

Summer 1814

The fact that the British needed to rely on contraband supplies from Vermont probably delayed the work on *Confiance* considerably. The size of the vessel increased the amount of time needed for completion, as it was the most ambitious vessel ever conceived for Lake Champlain. The shipbuilders at Isle Aux Noix did what they could, despite the American navy's efforts to cut off the flow of materials north.

That flow was considerable.

In late June, MacDonough's craft were pocketed near Windmill Point. The larger vessels were often to the west, near New York. The smaller ships and gunboats maneuvered south of Alburgh, near Isle La Motte, then over to North Hero and the southern reaches of Missisquoi Bay. Vessels embarked on irregular and random patrols.

During the first week of July, the boats stopped more processed wood bound for Canada, which again appeared to have been specifically cut for *Confiance*'s masts.[263] Rumors of who was involved spread across the Champlain Valley, and even some of the area's most prominent businessmen had their reputations tarnished by suspected involvement. Gideon King, the area's biggest ship owner and very likely involved in smuggling before the war, came under suspicion. He had originally sold many smaller craft to the American government, but during the summer of 1814, he was occasionally referenced as a notorious smuggler.[264] On July 23, yet another seizure was made. This time planks, spars and barrels of oil were caught floating north on rafts.[265]

The smuggling was not limited to the lake, and American commanders noted with frustration that stopping the flow of beef and cattle north was nearly impossible, especially on the Vermont border. General Izard, new to the area, quickly became educated on just how challenging the situation was. He noted at the end of July that there were so many herds of cattle moving through the woods that they made their own paths.[266]

July also marked an important level of activity behind the scenes, which played out just a few months later. The massive British effort to carry the war to the enemy was well underway. Just after July 4, while Americans quietly celebrated their independence, several British regiments departed from Europe. These were only a portion of the British buildup, but they were en route. They were the Third, Fifth, Twenty-Seventh and Fifty-Eight Regiments.[267]

The overall British plan was similar to one they had used before. English reinforcements would be used to descend through the Champlain Valley, using Lake Champlain as a knife to divide the northern colonies. Johnny Burgoyne's army got pretty far in the American Revolution before it was defeated at Saratoga.

In 1814, British assets in the southern United States were directed toward Washington and Baltimore, but the Champlain Valley would be the primary invasion route. As the British put into motion their plans around the nation's capital, and the first of their reinforcements arrived in Quebec, the American response in the Champlain Valley was…disorganized.

MacDonough responded to the threat of a large invasion by analyzing what Britain's naval capabilities already were and what they would become when *Confiance* sailed. His response was to petition the federal government for yet another large craft for the American fleet. If the British were coming, naval activity would be one of the prime factors in their effort. In early July, the shipbuilders at Vergennes began to descend upon the forests for white oak, the primary wood used in boat construction.[268]

Meanwhile, Izard brought most of the resources to Plattsburgh, where he essentially sat, knowing the War Department had not approved any offensive action. While the wait was deceptively calm, it prompted Izard's attention to turn to the Niagara Frontier. In Canada, Prévost had deceptively sent some of the first new units from Europe down to the St. Lawrence. The Americans fell for the ploy and believed the main thrust in the region would come farther to the west.[269] Throughout the early summer, there were dispatches between Plattsburgh and Washington, and finally, late in July, Izard received approval to take much of his army westward, where he thought it would confront the main British threat.

Prévost began to collect his growing army around Montreal, knowing that the timing depended on when enough of his forces could assemble near the shipyards at Isle Aux Noix. Any action depended on the control of the lake, and that revolved around completion of *Confiance*. Late in July, the Fifth, Twenty-Seventh and Fifty-Eighth Regiments disembarked from the ships that had carried them across the Atlantic onto Canadian soil.[270]

Things really came together for the British in August. They didn't for the Americans. Prévost, learning that *Confiance* was finally going to be done in early September, finalized his plans. He determined that invading through Vermont was not particularly advantageous. Certain elements of the Vermont population had traded with his army so much that in the event of a successful occupation of the Northeast, he did not want to turn the Vermonters against his soldiers.[271] He wrote to London that Vermonters were effectively feeding his army. This is perhaps the harshest and most clear indictment of disloyalty the people of the Green Mountain State showed during the War of 1812.

The Americans began to receive word of the larger than expected British forces to their north, but there is no indication that they changed their plans. Leadership still thought the bulk of the American forces should be moved to western New York. This strategy had huge repercussions for the Vermonters, who required an enemy ground invasion to convince them to defend their country. Izard finally appreciated the risks and attempted to have his orders changed, but Washington was half a continent away and did not change them.[272] Work that had started earlier in the summer, making Plattsburgh a truly defendable position, did receive more attention. The blockhouses along the Saranac River were restored, and work was hastened on three small forts being constructed along its southern bank.[273]

The broad plans the British had unfurled were well underway by late August, with an impressive amount of coordination between large forces at great distances. While Prévost inched toward the New York border and Lake Champlain, the southern forces struck in Washington on August 24. The capital of the United States was occupied, and many of the public buildings were burned. If the British wanted revenge against the rebellious colonies, it was a humiliating series of events for Americans. Izard tried to balance his military instincts with his orders. He moved the bulk of his forces out of Plattsburgh, set to move west during the last week of August, but left General Macomb and his brigade of approximately 1,100.[274] Macomb's relatively tiny force comprised the Sixth, Thirteenth, Sixteenth and Twenty-Ninth Regiments. Not long after Izard's untimely departure, Macomb received intelligence of the size of the approaching enemy just over the Canadian line. The low estimate had Prévost's army at about 7,000. Some reports were coming in that 14,000 English soldiers were just miles away.

On the lake, things were at least looking up for the Americans. The 120-foot brig, the *Eagle*, had been finished in Vergennes in an amazingly short amount of time. By August 1, MacDonough's counter to the *Confiance* was underway. With all the intelligence that *Confiance* was nearing completion, MacDonough brought his entire squadron north to Plattsburgh to survey the situation. At times, his position was off the northern end of Isle La Motte, just west of Blanchard's Point.[275] The ships patrolled north and south up to the border, but incidents that caused tensions between the locals and the military continued to unfold. While fears of invasion spread through the Champlain Valley, a particularly sad abuse occurred against American private citizens. If only a fraction of what happened on Isle La Motte is accurate, it is understandable why significant parts of the population did not favor the war.

Elements of the American fleet sounded the waters around Isle La Motte to investigate the possibility of a defensive position there. Such activity involved lowering ropes to the bottom of the lake to precisely measure the depth. It was discovered that the somewhat shallow waters near the island and relatively narrow waters to the west were not ideal defendable positions. While this tedious activity was happening, MacDonough, his officers and elements of the army and navy went ashore to check on and meet with the private citizens. MacDonough often called upon Captain Caleb Hill, who was in charge of the local militia. Tensions surfaced when questions came up about local militia having been involved in the smuggling while stationed in Swanton during the fall of 1812. Despite this, MacDonough called upon the Hills multiple times, earning the family's trust enough to arrange for food and supplies for the men on the boats under his command.

Some sailors didn't care for the arrangements MacDonough made. While the fleet was at anchor, men who wanted more than rations rowed to the island at night and stole what they needed. Chickens and livestock went missing, and many citizens found their gardens empty of produce.

Captain Hill confronted MacDonough on the night of August 16 and identified specific men and officers responsible for the activity. The meeting elevated into an argument, with MacDonough firmly stating that the men needed to be caught in the act. The response, while callous, is somewhat understandable. The navy had been having trouble getting men to serve throughout the war, and he didn't want to handcuff the operation of his ships without firm evidence. When Hill tried to provide the specifics, MacDonough insisted the men had to be caught in the act and suggested that Hill, as captain of the militia, needed to arrest them on the spot.

Later that evening, men from the fleet made their nightly raid into the town and specifically targeted the Hill household. They entered the home with muskets drawn and claimed to be English sailors looking for information on MacDonough's fleet. Hill attempted to draw his musket and was killed in his own kitchen. In the mêlée that followed, Arthur Hill, Caleb's son, barely survived a swinging sword, and received a wound along his face that scarred him for life.

The four or five guilty men were caught and a court-martial arranged, but they fled the navy before being charged. To alleviate tensions with the locals, MacDonough attended the funeral of Caleb Hill. Not long afterward, Arthur Hill was elected captain of the militia.[276]

Finally, Vermont got its chance to act heroically. Compared to the embarrassing amount of smuggling underway since before the war, Vermonters' actions contributed significantly to the fate of the British at Plattsburgh. It takes a lot to forgive treason. However, the events offered Vermonters a chance to say they left their villages, farms and families and confronted a much larger British army.

The actual size of that British army is open to historical debate. Many accounts place it at fourteen thousand men, but these numbers are probably on the high side. Historical investigations conducted in the late twentieth century reexamined much of the documentation available, and based on the size of all the known regiments involved, the true number is probably closer to ten thousand—and not all of them crossed the border. Prévost might have left a significant portion of his powerful army on the border as a reserve force.[277]

As the final British plans developed, MacDonough and Macomb met to determine the best use of the American navy. With the arrival of *Confiance* on the lake, MacDonough wasn't confident his vessels could challenge the enemy fleet in the open water. *Confiance* had more guns that could fire at a longer range. They determined the best place for the fleet was in Plattsburgh Bay, where the position gave the defending force a few small advantages. First, such a position allowed fire support against the enemy forces coming south as they entered Plattsburgh. Second, MacDonough hoped that an approach by the British would prove difficult, requiring them to maneuver slowly into position.²⁷⁸ The American vessels were not yet in position and would have to move into the bay.

Further analysis of the size of the force Vermonters were about to confront emphasizes the selfless, patriotic act about to be committed. The British army was organized into three brigades, consisting of many experienced soldiers from numerous regiments. Major General Robinson commanded the First Brigade. It was partially split when the invasion commenced, with portions of three regiments remaining on outpost duty. The rest of the brigade accompanied the invasion. The Second Brigade was headed by General Brisbane, and most of his soldiers moved over the border. The Third Brigade was made up of the Third, Fifth, Twenty-Seventh and Fifty-Eighth Regiments and was commanded by General Power.²⁷⁹ Thousands of experienced troops from the most powerful army in the world were about to invade the Champlain Valley.

The first push into New York occurred on August 30, when elements of the Second Brigade entered the town of Champlain. The Third and First Brigades moved into position, still in Canada. The New York militia was mustered, and MacDonough's navy was still north of the U.S. Army, relative to the lake. His vessels had their attention to the north, moving between Isle La Motte and Chazy.²⁸⁰ They would pull back into Plattsburgh Bay as the British ships began to move.

Most of the British infantry crossed the border on September 1. They moved slowly, knowing their fleet was not entirely ready. The gunboats, the sloops and the *Linnet* were primed and ready to go, cramped in the narrows of the lower Richelieu. The ground invasion expected support from the navy and would not thrust south until *Confiance* was ready. On the day when the British army entered New York, their prize ship was still being completed.²⁸¹

About seven hundred members of the northern New York militia rushed to defend Plattsburgh. Those coming from the south quickly went to the city, hoping to help with its defense. Macomb coordinated with General Mooers about how to best use the arriving reinforcements. Word went out to Vermont that its militia was desperately needed.²⁸² MacDonough dispatched the sloop *President* and all the bateaux that could be found to prepare for the hopeful participation of the Vermont militia. News of the burning of Washington arrived as the British were crossing the New York border. The news accounts descended upon the Champlain Valley, and New York and Vermont citizens knew something big was underway. The capital had been burned. A large British invasion force was entering the area only miles away.

The stark reality mustered a patriotic spirit in the men and women in the Champlain Valley.[283]

The British descent was slow, as the invasion force waited for the completion of *Confiance*. The army had crossed into New York at two different points. One branch proceeded into the village of Champlain and the other branch about a mile and a half to the east, along current Route 276. At this point, Prévost's generals urged a swift attack where the British army would lunge into Plattsburgh while the American defenses were still unorganized. The New York militia was just arriving, the army regulars were attempting to fortify their redoubts on the south bank of the Saranac and not a single Vermont unit had crossed the lake. *Confiance* was only a few days from completion. By September 4, the troops closer to the lake probably passed through Coopersville. The English army encamped near Chazy that night. Small units of New York militia obstructed roads and harassed the enemy just south of that town.[284]

Complementing the advance of the British army, the navy slowly moved south too. Most of the ships remained to the north, but six gunboats anchored off the northernmost point of Isle La Motte.[285] This particular action was in preparation for offensive activity on the island. The British wanted to occupy the west bank in support of their fleet. From that position, their

View of Windmill Point, Alburgh, looking north. British fleet traveled through this location prior to the Battle of Plattsburgh. *Photo by Armand Messier of northernvermontaerial.com.*

Northern Vermont in the War of 1812

View of Lake Champlain looking south from the Canadian border. Isle La Motte is on the horizon. *Photo by Armand Messier of northernvermontaerial.com.*

artillery could cover the advance of their ships and harass any American craft willing to confront the English navy north of Plattsburgh. Occupying this position was also a bit of a flanking maneuver, as it allowed a close eye to be kept on the Vermont towns of Alburgh and Isle La Motte. If any Vermonters were going to get involved, they would have to proceed much farther south to help defend Plattsburgh. Finally, the six gunboats could confront enemy ships coming up between the east bank of the island and Alburgh's southwest coast.

The two halves of the British army effectively linked up on September 5, in the general area of West Chazy, near Beekmantown. In Plattsburgh, the very first elements of Vermont militia were arriving, having departed the Vermont shore on whatever boats they could find. Vermont participation increased with the realization that Vermont soil was also under assault. At about this time, detachments of British soldiers packed on the six gunboats disembarked onto Isle La Motte and occupied parts of the island. Captain Pring, in command of the squadron of gunboats, ordered his men to find favorable land with a superior view of the south and construct a position for three big eighteen-pound cannons.[286]

Work quickly began on how to best use the island to their advantage. Chazy Landing, one of the temporary ports the British would use to offload supplies from their ships, lay just across the narrows of the lake, barely a mile away. As the redcoats took up their positions, they also scouted to assess if there were any elements of the Vermont militia still present. Pring ordered all privately owned firearms collected and handed over. His men constructed an embankment about a mile and a half south of Sandy Point (St. Anne's Shrine), and more heavy guns were unloaded. The position was hidden enough that American vessels wouldn't see it if they approach from the south. Trenches were dug around the embankment to provide further cover for the artillery and the troops. The house of John Manning was occupied near the artillery battery.

The order to collect the firearms of the residents who served in the militia was a practical one by the British, but it thrust many residents into a state of mini rebellion. The population was quite small, with barely six hundred at the time of the British landing. While there were many more men of fighting age than in the few British companies occupying, any organized opposition would have been difficult. Residents could see the entire British Navy resting off the northern shore, and the island's population was quite spread out. Individual landowners or farmers could do little against trained squads of the Crown's troops. Arthur Hill, the new captain of the militia, covertly gathered as many guns as possible to prevent British confiscation. He brought them to the east shore and hid them during the first night of the occupation. The next night, Hill and a few other residents took the guns and ammunition in a canoe to Alburgh, then North Hero and finally to Grand Isle.[287] Grand Isle was one of the rallying points for the Vermont militia as it moved to defend Plattsburgh. Tension rose on the islands as trained companies of British infantrymen occupied Isle La Motte and dozens and dozens of Vermont militia used Grand Isle as a staging area. The two forces were just a few miles apart. Isle La Motte was firmly in British hands. Vermont militia flowed across the lake just south of their position.

In New York, the British crept slowly south, and the first of many skirmishes unfolded on September 5. In a bold move, two companies of New York militia engaged the advanced pickets of the Third Regiment of Foot just a few miles north of Plattsburgh.[288] As the potential engagement drew near, Macomb ordered most of his sick, wounded and invalids onto Crab Island, in the southern portion of Plattsburgh Bay. There, Dr. Mann ministered to their needs as well as he could in wet weather. Some defensive cannon embankments were completed to offer fire support if the coming naval engagement should wander that far south. These men needed to be evacuated to Burlington, but there was little time to load and then unload

Northern Vermont in the War of 1812

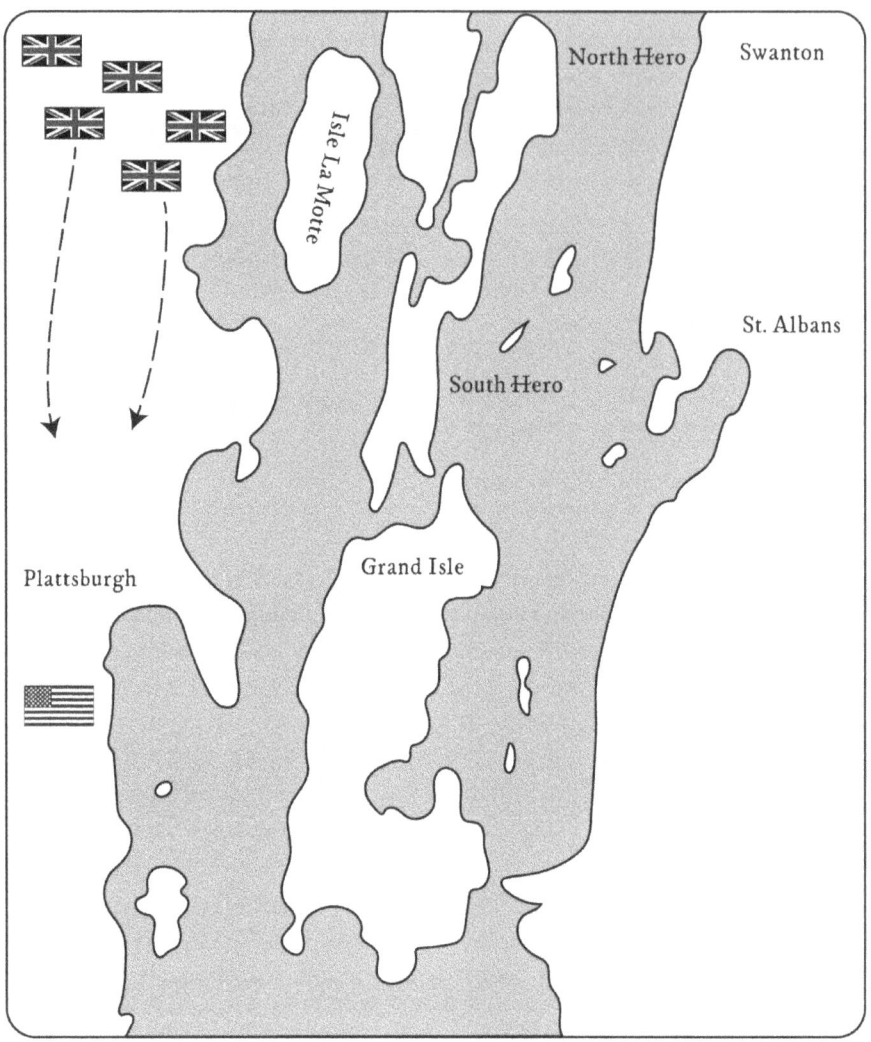

The British army approaches Plattsburgh in early September. *Artwork by Lindsay DiDio.*

them carefully. All the bateaux, the *President* and the smaller ships were making runs back to Vermont to bring over what militia they could.[289]

Further skirmishes occurred on September 6 when elements of the New York militia and a few companies of regulars, with two cannons, took up a position near the Ira Howe house in Plattsburgh. A significant firefight followed, and several British soldiers were wounded.[290] The Americans were able to use their cannons effectively for a short time. The British

Northern Vermont in the War of 1812

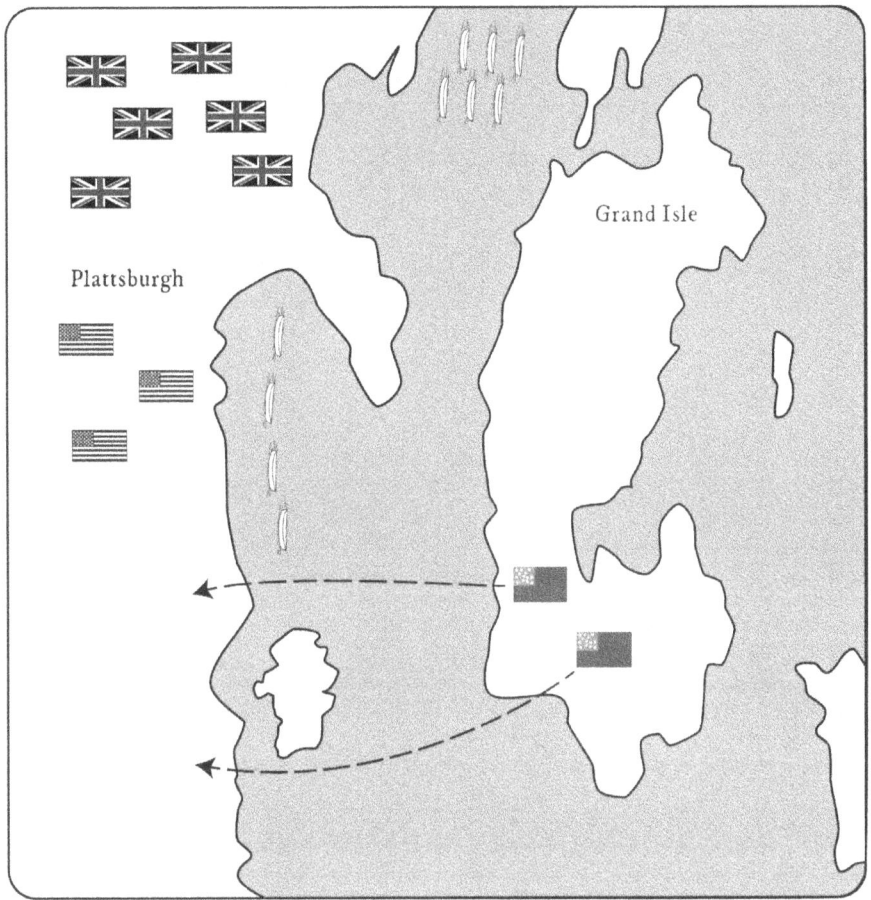

Vermont militia units from northern Vermont used Grand Isle as a rallying point. *Artwork by Lindsay DiDio.*

advance was not slowed, and soon the outnumbered Americans were forced to retreat.

By September 6, the redcoats were within a few miles of Plattsburgh, with the eastern portions of the army coming down the roads along the lake. As they marched in column toward Plattsburgh Bay, MacDonough's ships came into view. With the Americans retreating south of Beekmantown, elements of the army attempted a defense near the Saranac River. On the lake, with the British now in sight, MacDonough ordered several of his gunboats farther into the bay, along the coast, where they could support the defenders on land. Cannon fire from the gunboats temporarily halted the British along the lake, but the ships were dangerously exposed to enemy musket fire.[291]

For Vermonters, it was a moment of truth. One imagines a situation very much like Paul Revere's ride during the Revolutionary War, with horsemen riding from town to town exclaiming, "The British are coming! The British are coming!" And while they were not moving into Vermont, they were just a few miles away conquering American soil. The nation's capital had been burned. Word spread about the Isle La Motte occupation, and the first exchanges of fire were happening north of Plattsburgh. Large numbers of Vermonters answered the call.

While some had departed for New York immediately upon hearing the news of the British invasion, the first significant groups of Vermonters crossed the lake on the fifth and sixth of September. Volunteers under the command of General Strong were flowing into the encampments just south of the three redoubts. Not a significant number yet, but they were starting to arrive.

Some of the first were the men of St. Albans. Militia and volunteers from Swanton and other communities were not far behind. Most departed on horseback as quickly as they could, moving south through the towns of Georgia and Milton. At the sandbar, resting momentarily at Fox's tavern, they attempted to cross in the shallowest portions of the water, believing their horses could traverse locations that proved too deep. In their rush to get to Plattsburgh, the attempt failed, and they had to return to the Vermont shore. About another one hundred men had gathered, and the larger group successfully organized themselves into a line, making it easier to cross the lake. On the night of the sixth, this group reached a tavern on the western portion of Grand Isle, on the opposite side of the lake from Plattsburgh. While there, the owner of the tavern boldly told the group he hoped the British would prevail. The men responded that they were going to fight for their country.[292] The British occupation of Isle La Motte was underway just a few miles to the north. There, nervous militiamen scouted but did not challenge the British seizure of Vermont land.

Accounts of the Green Mountain Boys' departure from Grand Isle include references to a sloop coming to pick them up at around two o'clock in the afternoon, which provides incredible details into the razor-thin distances that separated the enemy forces. While the sloop was probably the *President*, every available ship was used in the effort. Operating between Grand Isle and Plattsburgh, the frenzied reinforcement attempt was underway literally within sight of the British navy at Isle La Motte. Macomb ordered the Vermont militia to assemble west of his forts, in the woods, on the south side of the Saranac River. American scout Eleazer Williams noted the arrival of one of the contingents from Franklin County in his journal.[293] By this point, the English were firmly in control of most of the territory north of the Saranac, with a good number of the buildings and homes in Plattsburgh either on fire, being used as defensive positions and taking fire, or smoldering, already having been burned.[294] The sight of large billowing columns of smoke was an eye opener for the Vermonters traversing the lake. What they went to defend was already in flames.

To the north, *Confiance* was essentially ready on September 7. There was still some carpentry being completed, and its gun crews were not yet ready, but the vessel left Isle Aux Noix to join the rest of the fleet. *Confiance* briefly ran aground just west of Alburgh as it was leaving the Richelieu. It was a momentary setback, and *Confiance* joined the fleet just off Isle La Motte on September 8.[295] While anchored there, the army and navy coordinated plans for when to dislodge the ragtag American forces assembling in Plattsburgh.

By this time the residents of Isle La Motte had been under occupation for approximately five days. It started with the arrival of the gunboats, but with each passing hour, the size of the fleet increased. With the British army in Plattsburgh, the Isle La Motte residents had an unwanted view of what was about to be thrown at MacDonough's navy, huddled south of Cumberland Head. The brigs *Confiance* and *Linnet* were the largest ships, followed by the sloops *Chub*, *Finch* and multiple other support vessels. As residents witnessed the militia units using Grand Isle as a staging area, they wondered if their tiny island might become part of the fighting.

At this point, British arrogance contributed to what was about to happen. In the narrow range of September 8 to the 10, they had multiple opportunities to swipe aside the American defenders in Plattsburgh and or bottle up MacDonough's navy in the bay. They did neither and waited for certain victory with the arrival of the *Confiance*.

Certain victory would cost them dearly.

On land, with nearly all the American forces retreating across the south side of the Saranac by September 8, Prévost could have sent elements around the American position, then come up from the south and the west. Such a move would have bottled up the Americans into a position where surrender was the only option.

Hesitating on the lake at this point cost the British dearly. The delay of twenty-four to forty-eight hours only complicated the land activity. Their fleet was at anchor between Chazy Landing and Isle La Motte. If they had shifted their strategy even a little and brought a portion of their flotilla just a few miles south, it would have had disastrous effects on the Vermonters valiantly crossing the lake. If the British had sent their gunboats south along Grand Isle and pushed even a little into the open lake, the reinforcements from Vermont would have ended in failure. The Vermonters would have been sitting ducks in their crammed bateaux, rowing across the lake. If those boats had been sunk, captured or retreated to the east, General Macomb would have been denied hundreds and hundreds of desperately needed soldiers.

The British wanted to defeat the Americans in one brilliant stroke. They believed the military would swipe aside the American army with little trouble and wanted it to happen on the same day the Royal Navy sunk the American ships. So confident were the British, they believed *Confiance* alone could take on the Yankee vessels.[296]

By the night of the eighth, the Saranac River separated the two armies. The Americans had engaged in a desperate attempt to make sure the bridges could not be crossed. The British now controlled most of Plattsburgh and slowed their advance. Prévost refused to push any advantage they had on land until his largest vessel could be brought into the fight on the lake.

The delay only allowed word to spread more widely in Vermont, and with each passing hour, growing numbers of Vermont militiamen showed up on the shores of Lake Champlain, waiting to catch any of the boats tirelessly ferrying forces across. The British army was over ten thousand men strong, and while the total number of Green Mountain Boys started to add up, there were only a few hundred gathered west of Macomb's forts, on the south bank of the Saranac.

On the river itself, there were no large engagements, only multiple smaller actions between the two armies. The British approached the river, tested American defenses and tried to find the best place to cross. On the American side, Macomb fully embraced the fog of war and ordered militia units to be as loud as possible. They moved around to various defensive locations, attempting to make the British think they were probing a much larger force.

On the Vermont side, certain communities became the hubs where Vermonters gathered to depart for New York. Charlotte, just south of Burlington, had several hundred men arrive from other towns to answer the call.[297] Every boat available was procured in the effort. Charlotte was likely the southernmost port used for the growing number of volunteers, although they came from everywhere.[298] A couple hundred volunteers departed from the Middlebury area, after ammunition had been collected all night. In some communities, it took time to organize enough men to form units, and there were delays in departing. In others, the response was immediate. Shelburne, another community with a dockyard on the lake, was another departure point—25 departed from there before a bottleneck formed behind them, and 43 left their homes in Jericho. Huntington, 25. Colchester, another coastal town, sent 37. Vermonters by the hundreds streamed across, all being ordered to shore up the American defenses along the Saranac. It continued all day on September 9 and increased on the following day. That night, General Strong reported to Macomb that by the morning of the eleventh there would be 2,500 Vermonters defending the Saranac River.[299] Meanwhile, many of the command officers of the British fleet dined and enjoyed drinks at Chazy Landing, believing that victory was mere hours away.[300]

Everything came to a head on the morning of September 11. The *Confiance* was finally ready, and the British fleet sailed south looking to engage the American fleet in Plattsburgh Bay. The movement immediately caused ripple effects across Lake Champlain, and the reinforcement effort screeched to a halt. With the *Confiance* and other ships underway, any small American craft either completed its last landing or returned to the Vermont shore. The men from Sheldon were one of the last groups to make it to New York that morning, before the advance of the British navy cut off the reinforcement route.[301] Hundreds of Vermonters were stranded on the Vermont side. Groups from Highgate weren't able to complete the same trek as those from Swanton and St. Albans had only two days before. Neither did those coming up from Rutland County. The men from Ira, Shoreham and Clarendon were unable to cross. At 7:00 a.m., the British fleet approached Cumberland Head and the last of the small American craft exited the area. The British were at Cumberland Head by 8:00 a.m.

The long-anticipated land and sea battle was finally at hand. Prévost was aware the fleet was underway and gave orders for elements of his army to move farther west and eject the defenders from their positions behind the Saranac. This was a worst-case scenario for the New York and Vermont militia, as their location would be one of the first attacked. Once the defenders along the Saranac were swatted away, the entire British force could push toward Lake Champlain and effectively squeeze Macomb and his men in the forts into submission.

British ground forces were moving into position as the Royal Navy entered Plattsburgh Bay. This was the moment that Prévost had waited for. His army had entered New York ten days ago, waiting for the navy, and now the two fleets were within sight of one another.

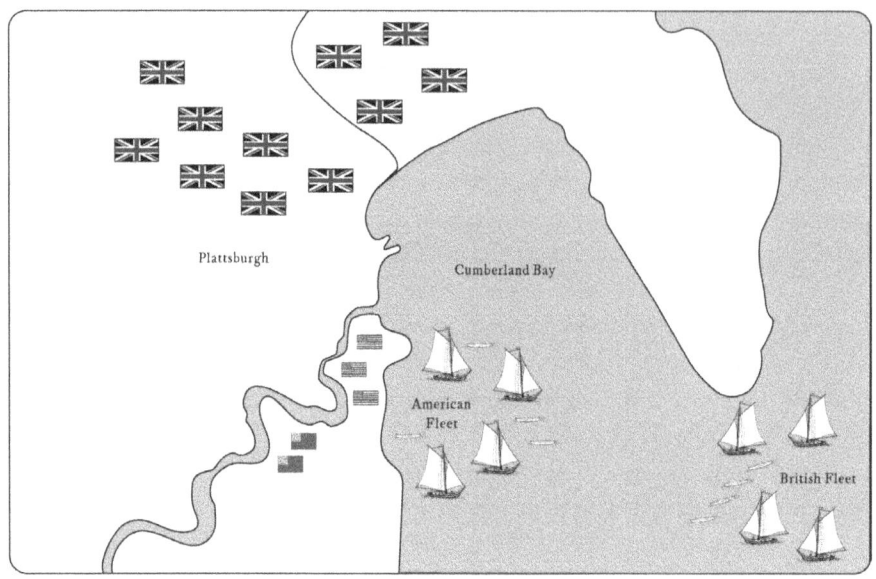

Prior to the Battle of Plattsburgh, the American fleet awaited the arrival of the English navy. *Artwork by Lindsay DiDio.*

As with the situation on land, the British believed that swiping aside the American fleet would be a relatively easy task. They believed that if they could maneuver all their vessels with their larger guns into position, it would be a short engagement. The British believed they would be able to round Cumberland Head, quickly sail into the bay and, with all their superior cannon, brush the American fleet aside.

A plan on paper is much different than reality, and the naval engagement began shortly after 9:00 a.m. Rounding Cumberland Head, the men working the British fleet saw the tops of the sails of the American vessels.[302] From the moment the British vessels entered the bay, they lost several advantages. The most notable was their inability to maneuver as swiftly as they wanted to once they were in the bay.[303] As the Royal Navy slowly closed in, MacDonough already had his ships in line waiting for them. The formation consisted of several gunboats to the north positioned somewhat behind the main vessels. From north to south, the *Eagle, Saratoga, Ticonderoga* and *Preble* lay waiting. Another group of gunboats anchored the American fleet against the northern tip of Crab Island, where a defensive battery had been established.

Testing the distance of the approaching enemy ships, the Americans fired first. The first shots were not effective, but as the British vessels crawled forward, they were able to strike the enemy. Before the Royal Navy was able to turn and launch its own broadsides, the fleet took heavy fire from the defending American vessels. On the north side of the line, *Confiance* took withering fire from the American gunboats, with the guns of the larger vessels only making the damage more significant. The British fleet hadn't been able to maneuver fast enough, and it was already taking critical damage. As the larger English squadron inched closer, the sailors turned to initiate their own broadsides with the enemy. However, the eddies and currents within Plattsburgh Bay played havoc with the ability of the British to bring their larger ships into position and seriously hampered their approach. These smaller gunboats wouldn't get close enough to participate in the volleys now being exchanged between the two fleets.[304] As firing commenced in earnest, curious onlookers from Plattsburgh, who had avoided the British pickets, watched from Cumberland Head. On the Vermont side, militia stranded on Grand Isle had a front-row seat to the unfolding action. Across the lake, residents from Chittenden County towns rushed to the shores of Colchester, attempting to catch views of the growing smoke and the increasing pounding of the cannons.[305]

MacDonough's defensive strategy worked masterfully. By the time all the British ships were in position to return fire, they had taken significant fire. Their own volleys were effective as well, with serious damage being inflicted on the American craft. During the first twenty minutes, the initial American fire caused havoc on the enemy. Two of the English vessels were effectively taken out of the fight. *Finch*, at the southern edge of the British line, took significant enough damage that it drifted away from the line into the fire of the defensive embankment on Crab Island.[306] Several British gunboats attempted to join the fray in this location, against *Preble* and *Ticonderoga*. To the north, the British vessel *Chub* was also taken out of the engagement when most of its rigging was blown away. A large complement of its crew was killed or wounded, and the vessel simply floated, not returning fire, into the American line.

Confiance and *Linnet* were able to get into position, but not as close as the battle plan initially called for. Had *Confiance* been able to maneuver quickly, set and engage, its fire alone would have been crippling. Once finally in position, the ship's cannons and those of *Linnet* were painfully effective. In the exchanges that followed, *Confiance*'s status as the most effective fighting vessel ever deployed on Lake Champlain resulted in great loss to the American vessels. The *Eagle* took crippling broadsides from both *Linnet* and *Confiance*. Partially because of the amount of damage it had sustained, the *Eagle* drifted south along the American line of ships. Naval tactics of the time involved vessels pivoting their ships around, presenting fresh guns and an undamaged side to the enemy. *Eagle* began this maneuver, but while doing so, *Confiance* and *Linnet* launched scorching shots against the *Saratoga*. The American fire was still effective enough though, and the commander of the British naval squadron, Downie, was killed. The broadsides continued, and MacDonough ordered *Saratoga* to turn and bring its fresh guns on *Confiance* as well.[307] The *Confiance* took blistering fire from *Eagle* and *Saratoga*, and by 10:30, its crew was having trouble keeping it afloat. By 10:50 a.m., the *Confiance*'s crew had struck their colors. With victory within their grasp, MacDonough ordered all the fire his fleet could muster onto the remaining *Linnet*. Just a few minutes later, the sole remaining British vessel, nearly crippled, surrendered. Shocked by the turn of events and not wanting to stand against the larger American vessels, the British gunboats retreated from Plattsburgh Bay into the lake just north of Cumberland Head.

Events on land would have little or no bearing on the outcome of the battle, except that the Vermonters had rallied against the British army and were willing to put up a spirited defense. That morning of September 11, they were huddled all along the Saranac River, spread out, waiting for the first British brigades to attempt to push south.

It never happened, at least to any great extent. The major land fighting involved exchanges between artillery batteries, particularly while troop movements occurred on the north side of the Saranac, while the British moved into position for their assault.[308] A hot spot that morning was the fire exchanged between the American redoubts and the British guns located to the north.[309] The British attempt to move south was initially successful, as it appears they were able to push across the Saranac near the location of Pike's cantonment. While historians disagree about the extent of the fighting on land that morning, recent primary source examination by Keith Herkalo and the Battle of Plattsburgh Museum suggests that the American retreat west of the redoubts was a planned fall back to a stronger location occupied by waiting artillery. New York and Vermont militia were both engaged with the British regulars, but it was more of an organized fallback with volleys designed to lure the British into an engagement with American cannon.

Although Isle La Motte was occupied by the British, that didn't stop the residents from doing what they could to support the American cause. On the day of the battle, the young Ira Hill had been asked to conduct a reconnaissance mission across the lake into British held territory, and he agreed. Unarmed, Hill crossed the lake and went a few miles into enemy lines, noting the location of support units, supply trains and general activity of the enemy.[310] The pullback likely began as Hill was on his way back to Vermont.

While the British pushed across the Saranac and tolerated militia sniping from behind trees, their advance came to a halt not long after the cannons on the lake had stopped firing. With the fleet out of action, Prévost had little enthusiasm for a bloody land campaign. By 3:00 p.m., he had given orders for a general retreat.[311] It was a stark and surprising turn of events, especially when the New York and Vermont militia moved north to keep an eye on the disinterested enemy.

On the lake, MacDonough's fleet kept an eye on the retreating British gunboats, and he assessed the damaged ships in the bay. The tally was shocking and reflected the intensity of the battle. *Finch* had taken 5 cannon balls to its hull, 3 striking below the waterline. It was the luckiest one. *Chub* had been struck 34 times. *Linnet* took at least 30. *Confiance*, the prize of the British navy, had been pummeled by over 250 shots to the hull.[312]

The organized British retreat wasn't a panic, but Prévost wanted to get out of American territory. Any equipment or supplies that broke down were ordered destroyed on the spot. The army and navy pooled their remaining resources at Isle La Motte and Chazy Landing, where ammunition, food supplies and support materials were packed onto the retreating ships. With the army trekking north, the vessels were still off Isle La Motte on September 12. MacDonough originally wanted his own gunboats to pursue the enemy fleet, but realizing the situation, he ordered them to monitor but not engage. The residents of Isle La Motte and the American gunboats witnessed an interesting scene as one of the smaller British sloops, a vessel originally seized from one of the residents of Grand Isle, was so packed full of supplies it took on water. Efforts to prevent it from sinking were futile, and the British abandoned the sloop and all the supplies. The people of Isle La Motte claimed the vessel and attempted to return it to its owner.[313]

On land, the retreat went mostly unchallenged, and heavy rain arrived while the British were hastily stumbling back toward the border, making any pursuit by the Americans just as difficult. The roads were mucky, and any push north would have involved a massive effort to move supplies and men. While the British retreated, a detachment of horsemen from Orwell, Vermont, challenged and captured the British southern pickets near Chazy Landing.[314] On the twelfth, the cleanup started, and some of the militiamen of Alburgh were ordered onto *Confiance* to remove the bodies. Two brothers of the Doty family were part of this group, and they saw the broken hull of the ship along with numerous bodies. Many of the deceased were taken to Crab Island and buried.[315]

With the army now crossing the border, the British navy skulked north and was soon at Isle Aux Noix. The American fleet kept eyes to the north, but with the loss of their largest vessels, the British did not have the capacity to challenge American control of Lake Champlain. Likewise, Macomb never gave serious consideration to pursing the British return to Canada, and the militia was quickly disbanded.

The Vermonters returned to their homes able to tell stories that had been sadly lacking on the eastern side of the lake throughout most of the war. They went home to Burlington, Vergennes, Swanton and dozens of other communities. In this one instance, they could claim Vermonters took on the British with duty, honor and sacrifice. They returned to their families, their crops and their home state. And they hoped that the war that had seized their lives for the last two years was finally over.

13
THE END

Fall, Winter, Spring 1814–1815

While the war was technically still on, there was very little activity of any consequence in the Champlain Valley after the Battle of Plattsburgh. That event acted as a crescendo after two long years of buildup, and the war was basically over by that point in time. Peace talks were underway. MacDonough repaired his vessels and those seized during the battle and brought them to patrol the northern edge of Lake Champlain. Prévost brought the English army back to Canada to lick its wounds. British leadership wondered how it was possible they had lost a second campaign through northern New York and New England. It is with great irony that events continued to go south for England through the fall and early winter. In spite of the many reinforcements that had arrived from Europe, after the burning of Washington, the tide of the war had taken a decidedly American turn. Prévost was not marching down the Champlain Valley linking up with other occupying armies. The British and Canadians had been able to hold the Americans at bay for two years. When the forces of the Crown finally went on the offensive, America earned its most impressive victories. Then peace was achieved. Word had not yet reached the southern theater, and the British commenced an attack against New Orleans in early 1815. Andrew Jackson and the American army were able to repel the enemy. The war was over, and America had earned another prominent victory.

14
THE PRESENT DAY

I'd like to thank The History Press for publishing this book. The investment in my research and willingness to publish it does bring me back to something that I mentioned earlier—the old saying that history is written by the victors. In this case, history is written by those who are interested, and there does seem to be a growing curiosity about local history topics. Perhaps documenting untold history is a better way to describe it.

All it takes is an idea. My admittedly intense childhood love of all things military morphed into the book you have today. I never would have been able to do my research or put together a book if I hadn't realized that the area I grew up in has one of the most unique backstories of anywhere in the United States.

Part of uncovering research is exploring the past, and I would like to take a moment to share with you what has been happening in Swanton to help build awareness of its own history. Around 2010, when I was doing a lot of master's-level professional development work for teaching, I was lucky enough to complete an internship with the Swanton Historical Society. That internship was to explore the town's War of 1812 history. I agreed to collect as much information as possible, going through primary and secondary source documentation. I presented the information at a venue where the community could learn about what I had uncovered.

The primary idea that sparked my interest in those early days was that, as a teacher, I might be able to provide a way for students to start uncovering real history. I loved history classes in high school and college. However, there

NORTHERN VERMONT IN THE WAR OF 1812

The Swanton Historical Society Depot. *Photo by Armand Messier of northernvermontaerial.com.*

is a growing school of thought that experiential learning is more engaging for students. The internship provided ample opportunities for me to expand my teaching, and at the time, the anniversary of the War of 1812 was approaching. People love anniversaries.

While the War of 1812 isn't even a focus of the Swanton Historical Society (it's trains), the community got the opportunity to learn and explore its own past. From 2010 to 2012, I put on a few public presentations that were well attended.

Getting others involved is still an issue I struggle with. As historians, we love history and we love the idea of uncovering something new. Something worthy. I don't think that is the case for most people.

A lot of people didn't even like school, and fewer still probably liked history class.

So, I used the story of 1812 and changed my teaching, and I think the results have been positive. Examples of this include efforts to organize historical walks along the route taken by the British in their August 1813 raid on Swanton. The Swanton history book provides a pretty good account, that they started at Maquam Bay, marched down Lake Road and crossed the Missisquoi River. As you learned, they then descended upon the town. Their return route was a little different. On numerous occasions, I either walked the invasion route or organized historical walking tours of those events for the Historical Society. I don't think there were too many people discussing the War of 1812 over family supper, but the events were nicely attended.

Another research and teaching focus became an effort to find the specific location of the barracks that the British torched in that attack. Author Keith Herkalo had success finding some of the encampments in Plattsburgh and that sparked interest in the 200th anniversary of the Battle of Plattsburgh in 2014. Given all the residential development in the places where the barracks was likely located, finding it was going to be a lot of work. Perhaps too much work for a high school history teacher to take on alone.

The community responded in positive ways, particularly local landowners who were willing to have their property investigated. We have undertaken as many as five different archaeological digs on various properties in Swanton Village. The digs were conducted by myself, Professor Scott McGlaughlin, students and teachers from Missisquoi Valley Union High School and helpful landowners. This last point cannot be stressed enough. The property owners who permitted archaeological digs allowed questions about history to be explored in meaningful ways. Unfortunately, as of this writing, the search for the barracks has not been successful.

The amount of residential development in Swanton over the last two hundred years has been substantial. The area in which the search is underway is the most densely populated section of the village. Finding the exact location of the barracks may never happen. We may find too much soil has been disturbed, too many cellars built, too many pools dug and too many driveways paved. Random chance appears to be the only factor to our benefit.

All is not lost, however. Local interest in the War of 1812 appears to be great enough that it will be covered in some detail at Missisquoi Valley Union High School, in the new Abenaki and Local History class. While this class may not be the spark that changes the world and brings on a generation of history fanatics, it will have a distinct focus on all things local. During the first semester it was offered there was only one section. In the second year, there were seven sections.

So, there is interest. And there is history to explore.

Thank you for reading.

NOTES

Chapter 1

1. Haviland and Power, *Original Vermonters*.
2. Perry/Barney, *History of Swanton*.
3. Ibid.
4. Ibid.
5. Nelson, *Benedict Arnold's Navy*.
6. Ibid.
7. Shattuck, *Insurrection, Corruption and Murder*, 30.

Chapter 2

8. Ibid., 33.
9. Ibid., 37.
10. Berry and Barney, *History of the Town*, 1007.
11. Everest, *War of 1812*, 10.
12. Shattuck, *Insurrection, Corruption and Murder*, 52.
13. Census 1791–1800.
14. Shattuck, *Insurrection, Corruption and Murder*, 75.
15. Stratton, *History, Town of Alburgh*.
16. Billings Special Collections, Wilbur, Penniman Letter 1808, Special Collections, University of Vermont Library.

17. Shattuck, *Insurrection, Corruption and Murder*, 102.
18. Ibid., 104.
19. Fairbanks, *Town of St. Johnsbury*, 165–68.
20. *New Bedford Mercury*, May 27, 1808.
21. Shattuck, *Insurrection, Corruption and Murder*, 106.
22. Ibid., 114.
23. Berry and Barney, *History of the Town*, 1963.
24. Shattuck, *Insurrection, Corruption and Murder*, 119.
25. Ibid., 124, 125.
26. Ibid., 135.
27. Muller, "Smuggling into Canada," 5–21.
28. Shattuck, *Insurrection, Corruption and Murder*, 137.
29. Hurd, *History of Clinton*.
30. Shattuck, *Insurrection, Corruption and Murder*, 139.
31. Hill, *History of Clinton*, 167.
32. Shattuck, *Insurrection, Corruption and Murder*, 282.
33. Ibid., 287.
34. Palmer, *History of Lake Champlain*, 165.
35. Bellico, *Sail and Steam in the Mountains*, 207.
36. Bassett, *Rise of Cornelieus Peter Van Ness*, 6.

Chapter 3

37. Berry and Barney, *History of the Town*, 1006.
38. Everest, *War of 1812*, 19.
39. Ibid., 37, 38.
40. Henderson, "Desperate Bravery," 2011.
41. Charbonneau, *Fortifications of Ile Aux Noix*, 130–37.
42. Hill, *Lake Champlain*, 165–67, 170.
43. Ibid., 172
44. Carton 1, Folder 10, Valentine Goodrich Letter, Colonel Isaac Clark Collection, Special Collections, University of Vermont Library.
45. Berry and Barney, *History of the Town*, 1006.
46. Valentine Goodrich Letter, Colonel Isaac Clark Collection, Special Collections, University of Vermont Library.

Chapter 4

47. Carton 1, Folder 32, Richford Selectboard Letter, Colonel Isaac Clark Collection, Special Collections, University of Vermont Library.
48. C. Clark, *Burlington Centinel*, July 4, 1812.
49. Lewis, *British Naval Activity*, 1.
50. Everest, *War of 1812*.
51. McLaughlin, personal communication.
52. Berry and Barney, *History of the Town*.
53. Pierre, *Invasion of Canada*, 1980.
54. Ibid.
55. *Plattsburgh Republican*, August 7, 1812.
56 Ibid.; Berry and Barney, *History of the Town*.
57. *Plattsburgh Republican*, September 4, 1812.
58. Ibid.
59. Everest, *War of 1812*, 64.
60. Ibid., 63.
61. *Plattsburgh Republican*, September 4, 1812.
62. *Washingtonian*, "From Troy," September 8, 1812, 3.
63. Lawson, "Fire by the Pond," 142–47.
64. Ibid.
65. Hay and Hay, *History of Derby*.
66. Ibid.
67. *Burlington Sentinal and Democrat*, Vermont Digital Newspaper Project, UVM Libraries, Bailey/Howe Library, http://library.uvm.edu/vtnp, accessed March 4, 2013.
68. Ibid.
69 Everest, *War of 1812*.
70 Johnson, *State of Vermont*, 1933.
71. Ibid.
72. Ibid.
73. Ibid.
74. Ibid.
75. "From Cook's Journal," *Washingtonian*, October 12, 1812.
76. "Plattsburgh," *Plattsburgh Republican*, September 17, 1812.
77. *Burlington Centinal*, Vermont Digital Newspaper Project, UVM Libraries, Bailey/Howe Library, accessed March 4, 2013, http://library.uvm.edu/vtnp.
78. Charbonneau, *Fortifications of Ile Aux Noix*.
79. Hurd, *History of Clinton and Franklin Counties*, 46.

80. Charbonneau, *Fortifications of Ile Aux Noix*, 147–52.
81. Lawrence, *History of Stanstead County*, 12.

Chapter 5

82. Bloomfield, *Bloomfield Pike Letterbook*.
83. "Military Records | Service Records | Ancestry.com," Search Historical Records–Ancestry.com, accessed March 5, 2013, http://search.ancestry.com/search/category.aspx?cat=39.
84. Everest, *War of 1812*, 64.
85. Fredriksen, *War of 1812*, 167.
86. Everest, *War of 1812*, 1981.
87. Herkalo, *Battles at Plattsburgh*.
88. Mann, *Medical Sketches* Dedham.
89. *Plattsburgh Republican*, October 16, 1812, http://news2.nnyln.net/plattsburgh-republican/search.html.
90. Special Collections, University of Vermont Libraries, Martindale Map, Bailey/Howe Library, http://library.uvm.edu/sc.
91. *Reports of Committees*, "Peter Bradley, Report 426," Committee on Invalid Pensions III, https://books.google.com/books?id=kKEFAAAAQAAJ&dq.
92. *Burlington Sentinal*, Vermont Digital Newspaper Project, UVM Libraries, Bailey/Howe Library, accessed March 4, 2013, http://library.uvm.edu/vtnp.
93. Edwin Ruthven Towle, "History of the Town of Franklin," RootsWeb.com, accessed March 5, 2013, http://www.rootsweb.ancestry.com/~vermont/FranklinFranklin.html.
94. Hickey, *War of 1812*.
95. Fredriksen, *War of 1812*.
96. "Plattsburgh," *Plattsburgh Republican*, October 23, 1812.
97. Ibid., October 30, 1812.
98. *Burlington Sentinal and Democrat*, 1812.
99. *Washingtonian*, 1812.
100. Berry and Barney, *History of the Town*, 1007.
101. Everest, *War of 1812*, 90.
102. *Burlington Sentinal and Democrat*, Vermont Digital Newspaper Project, UVM Libraries, Bailey/Howe Library, accessed March 4, 2013, http://library.uvm.edu/vtnp.
103. *Plattsburgh Republican*, November 6, 1812.
104. Everest, *War of 1812*, 90.

105. *Plattsburgh Republican*, November 26, 1812.
106. *Lansingburgh (NY) Gazette*, November 26, 1812.
107. *Plattsburgh Republican*, November 20, 1812.
108. Henderson, *War of 1812*, 2011.
109. Ibid.
110. "Third Invasion of Canada," *Washingtonian*, December 7, 1812.
111. "Colonel Stephen Pettis," Wing Library Guestbook, https://www.genealogy.com/ftm/w/a/g/Linda-Waggoner-CA/WEBSITE-0001/UHP-5899.html.
112. Berry and Barney, *History of the Town*.
113. Fredriksen, *War of 1812*, 174.
114. Johnson, *State of Vermont*.
115. "General Dearborn and the Northern Army," *Washingtonian*, December 14, 1812.
116. Colonel Isaac Clark Collection, Special Collections, University of Vermont Library.
117. Walton, *Records of the Governor*.
118 Bendal, "Montreal," 160.
119. "Montpelier," *Evening Post*, December 28, 1812.
120. "Third Invasion of Canada."

Chapter 6

121. Herkalo, *Battles at Plattsburgh*.
122. "Montpelier."
123. Ibid.
124. Ibid.
125. "Our Dying Troops," *Washingtonian*, December 21, 1812.
126. "Montpelier."
127. Everest, *War of 1812*, 93.
128. Graffagnino, *Vermont Voices*.
129. Shattuck, *Insurrection, Corruption and Murder*, 103.
130. Johnson, *State of Vermont*.
131. Swanton Cemetery Records.
132. Graffagnino, *Vermont Voices*.
133. Lawrence, *History of Stanstead County*, 74.
134. Colonel Isaac Clark Collection, Special Collections, University of Vermont Library.

Chapter 7

135. *Plattsburgh Republican*, March 26, 1813.
136. Everest, *War of 1812*, 103.
137. Berry and Barney, *History of the Town*.
138. "Gens D'Arms," *Washingtonian*, March 29, 1813.
139. "Case of Elisha Sears," *Washingtonian*, April 19, 1813.
140. Shattuck, *Insurrection, Corruption and Murder*, 291.
141. *Plattsburgh Republican*, 1812.
142. Ibid.
143. Palmer, *History of Lake Champlain*, 165.
144. Everest, *War of 1812*, 109.
145. Palmer, *History of Lake Champlain*, 165.
146. Everest, *War of 1812*, 109.
147. Bellico, *Sail and Steam*, 208.
148. Ibid., 209.
149. Bird, *Navies in the Mountains*.

Chapter 8

150. Shattuck, *Insurrection, Corruption and Murder*, 307.
151. Lewis, *British Naval Activity*, 8.
152. Ibid., 9.
153. Malcomson, *A to Z of the War of 1812*.
154. Auchinleck, "John Murray," in *History of the War Between Great Britain and the United States of America*, 204–5.
155. Malcomson, *A to Z of the War of 1812*.
156. Ibid.
157. Lewis, *British Naval Activity*, 1994.
158. "Calendar for Year 1813 (United States)," Timeanddate.com, accessed June 24, 2019, https://www.timeanddate.com/calendar/?year=1813&country=1.
159. Bellico, *Chronicles of Lake Champlain*.
160. Everest, *War of 1812*, 117.
161. Ibid.
162. *Inventory of the Town*.
163. Bellico, *Sail and Steam in the Mountains*, 210.
164. Bird, *Navies in the Mountains*, 282.
165. "Invasion," *Washingtonian*, August 4, 1813.

166. Ibid.
167. Bellico, *Chronicles of Lake Champlain*, 300.
168. Murray to Scheaffe, in Auchinleck, "John Murray," 204–5.
169. "Shameful Falsehood and Perjury," *Washingtonian*, August 30, 1813.
170. Berry and Barney, *History of the Town*.
171. Ibid.
172. "Shameful Falsehood and Perjury."
173. Ibid.
174. Berry and Barney, *History of the Town*.
175. Everest, *War of 1812*.
176. "Swanton," *Niles Weekly Register (Boston)*, August 28, 1813.
177. Ibid.
178. Malcomson, *A to Z of the War of 1812*.
179. *Lansingburgh (NY) Gazette*, August 31, 1813.
180. *Washingtonian*, 1812.
181. Everest, *War of 1812*, 126.
182. Ibid.
183. Johnson, *State of Vermont*.
184. Shattuck, *Insurrection, Corruption and Murder*, 311.
185. Everest, *War of 1812*, 121.
186. Lewis, *British Naval Activity*.
187. *Republican*, 1812.
188. Everest, *War of 1812*.
189. Karen Stites, "Isaac Clark, A Controversial Figure in Early Vermont History," UVM Special Collections, Burlington, May 17, 1987, reading.
190. Parker to Tatset, Colonel Isaac Clark Collection, Special Collections, University of Vermont Library.

Chapter 9

191. Everest, *War of 1812*, 128.
192. Little, *Loyalties in Conflict*.
193. *Lansingburgh (NY) Gazette*, October 26, 1813.
194. *Republican*, 1812.
195. Malcomson, *A to Z of the War of 1812*.
196. Clark, *Long Island Star*.
197. Darch and Racicot, "Distant Drum."
198. Ibid.

199. Little, *Loyalties in Conflict*.
200. Clark, *Long Island Star*.
201. "Prediction of a Warhawk," *Lansingburgh (NY) Gazette*, November 9, 1813.
202. Darch and Racicot, "Distant Drum."
203. Bowden, "Isaac Clark, Robert Searcy and James Colbert."
204. Bellico, *Sail and Steam*, 210.
205. Everest, *War of 1812*, 128.
206. Lewis, *British Naval Activity*, 17.
207. Everest, *War of 1812*, 129.
208. Shattuck, *Insurrection, Corruption and Murder*, 318.
209. Bellico, *Sail and Steam*, 211.

Chapter 10

210. Lawson, "Fire by the Pond," 141.
211. Maheaux, "Taplin."
212. Lawson, "Fire by the Pond."
213. Robinson, *Vermont*.
214. Lawson, "Fire by the Pond," 147.
215. Irving, *Officers*, 110, 199.
216. Hay and Hay, *History of Derby*, 49.
217. Little, *Loyalties*, 42.
218. Lewis, *British Naval Activity*, 17.
219. Bellico, *Sail and Steam*, 212.
220. Everest, *War of 1812*, 139.
221. Herkalo, *Battles at Plattsburgh*.
222. Fredriksen, *War of 1812*, 25.
223. Water, *Lake Champlain*, 250.
224. Henderson, "Patriots or Traitors."
225. Crocket, *Vermont*; Everest, *War of 1812*, 142.
226. UVM Special Collections.
227. Everest, *War of 1812*, 142; Water, *Lake Champlain*, 250.
228. UVM Special Collections.

Chapter 11

229. Fredriksen, *War of 1812*, 27.
230. Everest, *War of 1812*, 142.
231. UVM Special Collections, n.d.
232. Little, *Loyalties in Conflict*, 42.
233. Fredriksen, *War of 1812*, 27.
234. Everest, *War of 1812*, 142.
235. Fredriksen, *War of 1812*, 29.
236. Lewis, *British Naval Activity*.
237. Little, *Loyalties in Conflict*, 40, 41.
238. Fredriksen, *War of 1812*, 29.
239. Everest, *War of 1812*, 142.
240. Fredriksen, *War of 1812*, 29.
241. Henderson, "Desperate Bravery."
242. Fredriksen, *War of 1812*, 30.
243. Everest, *War of 1812*, 143.
244. Lewis, *British Naval Activity*, 19.
245. Ibid.
246. Bellico, *Chronicles of Lake Champlain*, 303.
247. Everest, *War of 1812*, 148.
248. Water, *Lake Champlain*, 253.
249. Lewis, *British Naval Activity*, 19, 20.
250. Ibid., 20.
251. Ibid., 20.
252. Bellico, *Sail and Steam*, 217.
253. Bellico, *Chronicles of Lake Champlain*, 303.
254. Lewis, *British Naval Activity*, 20.
255. Everest, *War of 1812*, 150.
256. Lewis, *British Naval Activity*, 21.
257. Bellico, *Chronicles of Lake Champlain*, 304.
258. Lewis, *British Naval Activity*, 23.
259. Herkalo, *Battles at Plattsburgh*, 57.
260. Bellico, *Chronicles of Lake Champlain*, 304.
261. Everest, *War of 1812*, 146.
262. Lewis, *British Naval Activity*, 26.

Chapter 12

263. Everest, *War of 1812*, 152.
264. Bellico, *Sail and Steam*, 218.
265. Everest, *War of 1812*, 152.
266. Bellico, *Sail and Steam*, 218.
267. Herkalo, *Battles at Plattsburgh*, 64.
268. Ibid., 64, 65.
269. Everest, *War of 1812*, 156.
270. Herkalo, *Battles at Plattsburgh*, 66.
271. Everest, *War of 1812*, 157.
272. Bellico, *Chronicles of Lake Champlain*, 305.
273. Ansley, *Vergennes in the War*, 20.
274. Herkalo, *Battles at Plattsburgh*, 67.
275. Stratton, *History, Town of Isle La Motte*.
276. Ibid., 53.
277. Everest, *War of 1812*, 167.
278. Fitz-Enz, *Final Invasion*, 88.
279. Everest, *War of 1812*.
280. Herkalo, *Battles at Plattsburgh*, 74, 76.
281. Lewis, *British Naval Activity*, 26.
282. Bellico, *Chronicles of Lake Champlain*, 307.
283. Fitz-Enz, *Final Invasion*, 103.
284. Everest, *War of 1812*, 169, 170.
285. Herkalo, *Battles at Plattsburgh*, 78.
286. Ibid., 80.
287. Stratton, *History, Town of Isle La Motte*, 53.
288. Fitz-Enz, *Final Invasion*, 108.
289. Everest, *War of 1812*, 279.
290. Ibid., 172.
291. Fitz-Enz, *Final Invasion*.
292. Hemenway, *Vermont Historical Gazetteer*, 342.
293. Herkalo, *Battles at Plattsburgh*, 96.
294. Ibid., 87.
295. Everest, *War of 1812*, 179.
296. Herkalo, *Battles at Plattsburgh*, 97.
297. Ibid., 98.
298. Everest, *War of 1812*, 177.
299. Fitz-Enz, *Final Invasion*, 132.

300. Bellico, *Chronicles of Lake Champlain*, 309
301. Aston, *Sheldon*.
302. Bellico, *Chronicles of Lake Champlain*, 309.
303. Ansley, *Vergennes in the War*, 9.
304. Everest, *War of 1812*, 181.
305. *History of Colchester*, 54.
306. Bellico, *Chronicles of Lake Champlain*, 311.
307. Water, *Lake Champlain*, 266.
308. Everest, *War of 1812*, 187.
309. Herkalo, *Battles at Plattsburgh*, 115.
310. Stratton, *History, Town of Isle La Motte*, 55.
311. Everest, *War of 1812*, 137.
312. Herkalo, *Battles at Plattsburgh*, 121.
313. Stratton, *History, Town of Isle La Motte*, 54.
314. Everest, *War of 1812*, 189.
315. Bellico, *Chronicles of Lake Champlain*, 316.

BIBLIOGRAPHY

Ansley, Norman. *Vergennes in the War of 1812*. Severna Park, MD: Sheridan Press, 1999.
Aston, Dorothy Hemenway. *Sheldon, Vermont*. Saint Albans, VT: Regal Arts Press, 1979.
Auchinleck, Gilbert. *A History of the War Between Great Britian and the United States of America during the years 1812, 1813, and 1814*. Toronto: Palala Press, 1972.
Bassett, Seymour. *The Rise of Cornelieus Peter Van Ness*. Barre: Vermont Historical Society, 1942.
Bellico, Russell. *Chronicles of Lake Champlain*. Fleischmanns, NY: Purple Mountain Press, 1999.
———. *Sail and Steam in the Mountains*. Fleischmanns, NY: Purple Mountain Press, n.d.
Bendal, Betty. "Montreal." *Vermont Quarterly* 22 (1954): 160
Berry, John B., and George Barney. *The History of the Town of Swanton*. Salem, MA: Higginson Book Company, n.d.
Bird, Harrison. *Navies in the Mountains*. New York: Oxford Press, 1962.
Bloomfield, Joseph. *Bloomfield Pike Letterbook*. Ann Arbor, MI: William L. Clements Library, 1812.
Bowden, Mary. 2013. "Isaac Clark, Robert Searcy and James Colbert: In Their Own Words." Headliners Foundation. Accessed July 2018. https://www.headlinersfoundation.org/latest-news/2018/12/17/isaac-clark-robert-searcy-and-james-colbert-in-their-own-words.

Bibliography

Census, 1790/1800. https://www.familysearch.org/search/collection/1803959 and https://www.familysearch.org/search/collection/1804228.

Charbonneau, Andre. *The Fortifications of Ile Aux Noix*. Ottawa: Ministry of Supply and Services Canada, 1994.

Clark, Colonel. *Burlington Centinel*, July 4, 1812.

Clark, Isaac. *Long Island Star*, November 3, 1813.

Crockett, Walter Hill. *A History of Lake Champlain, 1609–1909*. Burlington, VT: Hobart, Shanley & Company, 1909.

———. *Vermont, the Green Mountain State*. 4 vols. New York: Century History, 1921.

Darch, Heather, and Michel Racicot. "A Distant Drum: The War of 1812 in Missisquoi County." *Townships Heritage WebMagizine*. http://townshipsheritage.com/article/distant-drum-war-1812-missisquoi-county.

Everest, Allan. *The War of 1812 in the Champlain Valley*. Syracuse, NY: Syracuse University Press, 1981.

Fairbanks, Edward T. *Town of St. Johnsbury, Vermont*. St. Johnsbury, VT: Cowles Press, 1914.

Farfan, Matthew, ed. *Townships Heritage Web Magazine*. Accessed July 19, 2018. http://townshipsheritage.com/about-townships-heritage-webmagazine.

Fitz-Enz, David G. *The Final Invasion*. New York: Cooper Square Press, n.d.

Fredriksen, John C. *The War of 1812 in Person*. Jefferson, NC: McFarland, 2009.

Goodrich, Valentine. n.d. *Goodrich to Clark*. Burlington, UVM Special Collections.

Graffagnino, J. Kevin. *Vermont Voices: 1609 through the 1990s*. Barre: Vermont Historical Society, n.d..

Haviland, William, and Marjory W. Power. *The Original Vermonters*. Hanover, NH: University Press of New England, 1994.

Hay, Cecile B., and Mildred B. Hay. *History of Derby*. Vermont Civil War Enterprises, 1998.

Hemenway, Abby, ed. *The Vermont Historical Gazetteer: A Magazine, Embracing a History of Each Town, Civil, Ecclesiastical, Biographical and Military, Volume 2*. Burlington, VT: n.p., 1871.

Henderson, Robert. "Desperate Bravery." War of 1812. http://www.warof1812.ca/lacolle.htm.

———. "Patriots or Traitors, The Leaking of Secret U.S. War Plans." War of 1812. http://www.warof1812.ca/patriotstraitors.htm.

Herkalo, Keith. *The Battles at Plattsburgh*. Charleston, SC: The History Press, 2012.

Hickey, Donald R. *The War of 1812: A Forgotten Conflict*. Urbana: University of Illinois Press, 1989.

Hill, Ralph Nading. *Lake Champlain Key to Liberty*. Montpelier: Vermont Life Magazine, 1995.

Hurd, D. Hamilton. *History of Clinton and Franklin Counties, New York: With Illustrations and Biographical Sketches of Its Prominent Men and Pioneers*. Philadelphia: J.W. Lewis, 1880.

Inventory of the Town, Village and City Archives of Vermont, No. 7, Towns of Grand Isle County. Montpelier, VT: The Survey, 1938.

Irving, L. Homfrey. *Officers of the British Forces in Canada During the War of 1812*. Sligo, IRL: Hardpress, 1908.

Johnson, Herbert T. *State of Vermont, Roster of Soldiers in the War of 1812–14*. St. Albans, VT: Messenger Press, 1933.

Lawrence, John. *The History of Stanstead County, Quebec*. Montreal: Lovell Printing and Publishing Company, 1874.

Lawson, Kenneth. "A Fire by the Pond: The British Raid in Derby, Vermont, December 27, 1813." *Vermont History* 80, no. 2 (Summer/Fall 2012): 141–57. vermonthistory.org/journal/80/VHS8002BritishRaid.pdf.

Lewis, Dennis. *British Naval Activity On Lake Champlain During the War of 1812*. New York: Clinton County Historical Association/Essex County Historical Society, 1994.

Little, John. *Loyalties in Conflict*. Toronto: University of Toronto Press, n.d.

Maheaux, Joseph. "Taplin." *Stanstead Historical Society Journal*, no. 5 (1973): 27.

Malcomson, Robert. *The A to Z of the War of 1812*. Lanham, MD: Scarecrow Press, 2006.

Mann, James. *Medical Sketches*. Dedham, MA: H. Mann and Company, 1816.

McLaughlin, Scott. Personal communication with the author. 2013.

Muller, H.N. "Smuggling into Canada: How the Champlain Valley Defied Jefferson's Embargo." *Vermont History* 38, no.1 (Winter 1970): 5–21.

———. "A 'Traitorous and Diabolical Traffic': The Commerce of the Champlain-Richelieu Corridor During the War of 1812." *Vermont History* 44, no. 2 (Spring 1976): 78–96.

Nelson, James. *Benedict Arnold's Navy*. New York International Marine Publishing, 2006.

Palmer, Peter S. *History of Lake Champlain, from Its Exploration by the French in 1609 to the Close of the Year 1814*. New York: Frank F. Lovell and Company, n.d.

Penniman, Jabez. 1808. "Nathan Haswell Papers, UVM." Billings Special Collections Wilbur, University of Vermont, Burlington, Vermont.

———. 1808. "Penniman Letter." Haswell Papers, 1805–1810, UVM.

BIBLIOGRAPHY

Perry/Barney. *The History of Swanton.* Swanton, VT: Hemingway, 1882.

Pierre, Burton. *The Invasion of Canada.* Toronto: McClelland and Stewart, 1980.

Plattsburgh Centenary Commission. *The Battle of Plattsburg: What Historians Say About It.* Albany, NY: Lyon, 1914.

Robinson, Rowland E. *Vermont, A Study in Independence.* Boston: Houghton Mifflin, 18992.

Shattuck, Gary. *Insurrection, Corruption and Murder in Early Vermont.* Charleston, SC: The History Press, 2014.

Stahl, John M. *The Battle of Plattsburgh: A Study of the War of 1812.* Argos, IN: Van Trump Company, 1918.

Stratton, A.L. *History, Town of Alburgh, Vermont.* Madison: University of Wisconsin Press, 1982.

———. *History, Town of Isle La Motte.* Madison: University of Wisconsin Press, 1984.

Swanton Cemetery Records, report/index, Swanton Historical Society, Swanton, Vermont.

UVM Special Collections. UVM Bailey Library. Accessed 2013.

Walton, E.P. *Records of the Governor and Council of the State of Vermont.* Montpelier, VT: J.&J.M. Poland, 1878.

Water, Frederic Van De. *Lake Champlain and Lake George.* New York: Bobbs Merrill Company, 1946.

Wilbur, Lafayette. *Early History of Vermont.* Jericho, VT: Roscoe Printing Press, 1902.

Wright, Ruth. *Colchester Vermont from Ice-cap to Interstate.* N.p., 1963. Print copy in the collection of the Burnham Library, the public library of Colchester, Vermont.

INDEX

A

Ackley, Joel 82
Adams 60
Alburgh 18, 21, 23, 26, 28, 29, 30, 32, 38, 40, 62, 63, 66, 67, 69, 76, 80, 82, 83, 95, 98, 99, 108, 120, 122, 123, 126, 127, 134, 135, 139, 145
Alert, customs vessel 108
Alwyn, gunboat 107
Asselstyne, Candis 93
Austin, Rufus 58

B

Ballard, gunboat 107
Barney, Rufus 95
Barns, Hezekiah 46
Baynes 44, 45, 49
Beaumont, Dr. William 72
Beaver, schooner 31
Beekmantown 134, 137
Beresford 55, 77
Berkshire 24, 60
Bigsby, Samuel 72
Billings, Captain 62
Bingham 60
Black Snake 30, 31, 32, 33, 41, 46
Blanchard, Orlin 82, 83, 86, 93
Bloomfield 50, 51, 57, 59, 60, 62, 72
Bodwell, Lieutenant 111
Bouquet River 123, 124
Boynton, Ensign 111
Bradley, Peter 60
Briggs 60
Brisbane, General 132
Brock 55, 77
Broke 78, 79, 80, 83, 85, 121, 123
Brooks, Eleazer 93
Brown 60
Brown, Amasa 95
Brown, Stephen 95

INDEX

Bulldog, sloop 66, 70, 76
Burlington 15, 17, 24, 26, 28, 33, 36, 37, 40, 43, 48, 50, 51, 52, 53, 57, 58, 60, 61, 62, 67, 69, 70, 71, 73, 74, 75, 78, 80, 82, 83, 85, 92, 94, 95, 103, 109, 112, 114, 115, 117, 122, 124, 135, 140, 146
Burlington Packet 82, 86
Burnap 60
Burt, Augustus 91
Burtonville 39

C

Caldwell's Manor 31, 114
Canada, sloop 96, 108, 123, 124
Carley, Joel 89
Cassen, Fort 122, 124
Charlotte 30, 46, 140
Chateaugay 94, 96, 98, 105, 107, 114
Chub, sloop 123, 139, 143, 145
Clark, Isaac 50, 61, 62, 66, 69, 72, 86, 91, 96, 97, 98, 99, 102, 104, 111, 115, 116, 117, 119
Colchester 85, 141, 143
Confiance 125, 126, 127, 128, 129, 130, 131, 132, 133, 139, 140, 141, 143, 144, 145
Coopersville 133
Crab Island 135, 142, 143, 146
Cross 60
Cumberland Head 82, 95, 108, 123, 126, 139, 141, 142, 143, 144
Curtis, Captain 111

D

Dean, Cyrus B. 33
Dearborn, General 51, 58, 59, 61, 62, 63, 66, 67, 72
Derby 44, 50, 51, 53, 60, 62, 63, 78, 110, 111, 120
De Salaberry, Major Charles 38
Dixon, Luther 94, 97
Dodge, Andrew 53, 69
Downie 144
Duclos, Francis 38, 114
Durkee 53, 69

E

Eagle, 1814 130, 142, 143
Eagle, sloop, 1811 34
Eagle, sloop, 1813 76, 77, 79
Edson, Lieutenant 75
Embargo Acts 27
Embodied Militia 36, 66, 80, 102
Emery, Samuel 95
Enosburgh 24, 52
Enterprise 34, 86
Essex County Militia 124
Essex, New York 30, 78
Essex, sloop 1811 34
Essex, sloop 1813 86
Essex, Vermont 85
Euretta 34
Everard, Captain 80, 83

F

Farrington, Lieutenant 32
Federal Victory 86
Fencibles 36, 66, 80
Ferry Street 62, 90

Fifield, Colonel 52, 60, 61, 62, 65, 67, 69, 72, 73, 74, 75, 111
Finch, sloop 123, 139, 143
Fly, revenue cutter 30, 32, 33, 40
Fox, sloop 34, 50, 62
Frances, sloop 78, 95, 99, 112, 125
Franklin, county of 27, 40, 43, 46, 69, 72, 95, 139
Franklin, town of 24, 63
Frelighsburg 102, 104
French Mills 113
Frimmer, Nicholas 58

G

Galusha, Jonas 40, 43
Georgia 138
Goodrich, Ezekiel 95
Goodrich, Valentine 40, 41, 46, 57, 58, 91, 92, 95
Gordon, Captain 80
Grand Isle 28, 46, 52, 104, 123, 135, 138, 139, 140, 143, 145
Growler 76, 77, 79

H

Hall, Cobb 60
Hampton, General 80, 94, 95, 96, 102, 107
Haswell, Nathan 29, 79, 115
Hathaway, Shadrack 95
Highgate 22, 24, 27, 46, 51, 52, 54, 78, 101, 104, 112, 120, 141
Hill, Arthur 131, 135
Hill, Caleb 43, 83, 130, 131
Hinesburg 31
Holly, Paul 60
Hopkins 60
Hotchkiss 60
Hubbard, John 75
Hunter, sloop 34, 50, 57, 62, 70, 76
Huntington 141
Huntsburgh 63, 75, 104

I

Icicle, sloop 96, 123, 124
Independence 34
Isle Aux Noix 39, 53, 54, 55, 60, 61, 63, 66, 76, 77, 79, 80, 86, 95, 98, 108, 112, 113, 114, 115, 117, 118, 120, 121, 122, 123, 124, 125, 126, 127, 129, 139, 146
Isle La Motte 31, 63, 82, 83, 86, 93, 95, 99, 108, 127, 130, 133, 135, 138, 139, 144, 145
Izard, General 122, 123, 128, 129, 130

J

Jericho 141
Juno, sloop 31, 34, 40, 50, 76, 78
Jupiter, sloop 34, 50, 78

K

Kendall, George 44, 46
King, Gideon 34, 127

L

Lacolle Mills 55, 96, 120
Lady Washington 34
Lake Champlain 27, 28, 32, 37, 42, 44, 45, 48, 51, 57, 58, 61, 62,

INDEX

68, 76, 78, 80, 93, 96, 107, 112, 115, 124, 126, 129, 140, 141, 146, 147
Lamphiere, John 57
Lark 33, 40, 86
Linnet 112, 115, 120, 122, 123, 125, 132, 139, 143, 144, 145
Loomis 77
Lowry 44, 46
Ludlow, gunboat 107
Luke, Colonel 102
Lynde, Cornelius 72

M

MacDonough, Thomas 58, 70, 76, 78, 80, 81, 82, 84, 85, 86, 95, 107, 108, 109, 112, 113, 115, 122, 123, 124, 125, 126, 127, 128, 130, 131, 132, 137, 139, 142, 143, 144, 145, 147
Macomb, General 114, 115, 116, 117, 119, 120, 122, 123, 129, 130, 131, 132, 135, 138, 140, 141, 146
Macon's Bill No. 2 27
Mann, Dr. Charles 59, 71, 113, 135
Manzer 87, 93, 95
Manzer, Abraham 95
Maquam Bay 26, 32, 63, 83, 86, 149
Mars, sloop 34, 86, 96
Martindale, Colonel 52, 60, 69
Mason, Hiram 53, 60
McFeely, Colonel 114, 115, 117, 118, 119
Memphremagog 50, 69, 111, 120
Messa, Lieutenant 111

Middlebury 40, 140
Missisquoi Bay 24, 29, 31, 32, 38, 46, 55, 61, 62, 69, 86, 97, 99, 102, 103, 104, 107, 108, 116, 117, 120
Missisquoi River 18, 19, 21, 22, 24, 26, 30, 31, 40, 62, 63, 67, 86, 87, 89, 92, 149
Mohawks, Kahnawake 66
Montgomery, sloop 78, 95, 99, 112, 125
Montpelier 40, 43
Montreal 26, 37, 39, 45, 51, 55, 59, 61, 66, 69, 74, 79, 80, 98, 113, 114, 118, 122, 129
Moore, Pliny 107, 108
Morrill 53, 73
Murray, Colonel 80, 81, 82, 86, 87, 89, 92, 94, 95, 99, 125, 156, 157

N

Needham 60
Non-Intercourse Act 27
North Hero 63, 83, 99, 127, 135
Northrup, Wanton 92
Noyce 60

O

Odelltown 53, 121
Old Brick Store 91
Ormsbee 60
Orwell 145
Otter Creek 112, 115, 122, 123, 124

INDEX

P

Parker, John 82, 83, 86, 93, 97
Parson 60
Penniman, Jabez 28, 29, 31, 32, 33, 40, 91
Perrault, Major 107
Pettis, Cindy 67
Pettis, Stephen 44, 46, 67
Phelps, Matthew 46, 58
Phillipsburg 63, 102, 117
Pike, Zebulan 50, 66, 72, 81, 144, 154, 163
Popham 55, 77
potash 24, 25, 26, 30, 32, 42
Powell, Major 102
Preble 78, 95, 99, 112, 125, 142, 143
President, sloop 50, 58, 62, 66, 70, 76, 78, 95, 99, 108, 112, 125, 132, 136
Preston 60
Prévost, Governor General 36, 37, 38, 44, 45, 55, 56, 59, 73, 78, 79, 80, 128, 129, 130, 131, 133, 139, 140, 141, 145, 147
Pring, Captain 80, 83, 123, 124, 134

R

Red Bird 86
Richard, sloop 34
Richardson 60
Richelieu 18, 20, 21, 22, 27, 28, 30, 37, 38, 39, 44, 54, 55, 56, 66, 76, 77, 95, 98, 108, 113, 119, 121, 126, 132, 139

Richford 24, 40, 43, 44, 52, 60, 70, 73
Rising Son 34, 78
Robbins 44, 46
Robinson, Major General 132
Robinson, Senator 117
Rock River 101, 104
Rouses Point 18, 38, 62, 63, 66, 120, 122, 123, 126
Rutland 30, 31, 141

S

Sabin 60
Sailly, Peter 122
Saranac River 60, 81, 129, 137, 138, 140, 141, 144
Saratoga, ship, 1814 123, 125, 144
Saxe, Conrade 46, 51
Saxe, Matthew 82
Scott, Captain John 58, 61
Scott, Levi 87
Scoville 60
Sears, Elisha 75
Shannon 78
Shelburne 70, 85, 141
Sheldon 24, 28, 38, 114, 141
Smith, Lieutenant Sidney 49, 58, 60, 62, 77
Sowles, Mr. 92
St. Albans 30, 31, 87, 92, 138, 141
Stanstead 51, 56, 70, 111
St. Armand 53, 54, 63
Stewart, Reverend 102
Strait 60
St. Regis 62, 96

INDEX

T

Taplin, Captain 111
Tatset, Elias 97
Taylor, James 44, 46, 53, 72
Ticonderoga, ship, 1814 123, 125, 142, 143
Toby, Captain Edward 73
Treadwell, James 96

V

Vergennes 71, 112, 122, 123, 124, 126, 128, 130, 146
Voltigeurs 36, 38, 66

W

Walker, Enos 53
Washingtonian, the 69, 71, 75, 93
Wasp, sloop 78, 80, 95, 99, 112, 125
West Chazy 134
Wheatley 53, 69
Wheeler 53, 69
Whitehall 49, 50, 58, 62, 66
Wilkinson, General 94, 98, 102, 107, 113, 114, 115, 116, 118, 119, 120, 121, 122
Williams, Jonathan 52, 60
Williams Regiment 46, 60
Willing Maid 86
Wilmer, gunboat 107
Wilson, Boswell 44, 45
Windmill Point 28, 31, 33, 63, 80, 108, 126, 127
Wood, Dr. James 33, 80, 83
Wright, Simeon 60, 69

ABOUT THE AUTHOR

Jason Barney grew up in northern Vermont and received a public school education. His interest in history started at Highgate Elementary when he was just a kid. While he loved social studies classes at that early age, he also fondly remembers his father and grandfather keeping binders of Barney genealogy information. What started out as an intense interest in the American Civil War and World War II turned into a love of high school history class. He looks back on the social studies classes of Missisquoi Valley Union High School and believes those were the sessions where his own desire to be a teacher was crafted.

Jason graduated from high school in 1993 and attended the College of Saint Joseph's in Rutland, Vermont. The history classes in college were more in-depth, more detailed and a lot of fun. Jason completed the necessary requirements to become a teacher.

Prior to embracing a career in education, Jason ran for public office. Between the years of 1997 and 2002, Jason represented the Towns of Franklin and Highgate in the Vermont House of Representatives. When he left the legislature, he had attained the position of vice chairman of the Education Committee.

He moved into education and substitute taught at the schools in northwestern Vermont before being hired as a full-time teacher at the high

About the Author

school he graduated from. The longer he teaches, the more he likes it. His intense interest in local history began when he was invited to be a member of the Swanton Historical Society.

Presently, he lives in northwest Vermont with his wife, Christine Eldred, and son, Samuel. They own three acres not too far from Lake Champlain. Jason loves to garden, read, write and teach. He is a huge New England Patriots fan. Jason spends part of his free time reading and taking notes on Star Trek books, helping to maintain the Star Trek Timeline by Pocket Books. He is forty-three years old.

Visit us at
www.historypress.com

www.ingramcontent.com/pod-product-compliance
Lightning Source LLC
Chambersburg PA
CBHW042140160426
43201CB00021B/2349